W9-BYG-117

Cacti & Succulents

Hans Hecht

Sterling Publishing Co., Inc. New York

Library of Congress Cataloging-in-Publication Data

Hecht, Hans.
    [Kakteen und andere Sukkulenten. English]
    Cacti & succulents / Hans Hecht.
        p.   cm.
    Includes index.
    ISBN 0-8069-0548-4
    1. Cactus.   2. Succulent plants.   3. Cactus—Pictorial
works.   4. Succulent plants—Pictorial works.   I. Title.   II. Title:
Cacti and succulents.
    SB438.H413   1994
    635.9'3347—dc20
                                                            93-44069
                                                              CIP

10   9   8   7   6   5   4   3   2   1

Published in 1994 by Sterling Publishing Company, Inc.
387 Park Avenue South, New York, N.Y. 10016
Originally published and © 1992 by
Mosaik Verlag GmbH, München, Germany
under the title *Kakteen und Andere Sukkulenten*
English translation © 1994 by Sterling Publishing Co., Inc.
Distributed in Canada by Sterling Publishing
℅ Canadian Manda Group, P.O. Box 920, Station U
Toronto, Ontario, Canada M8Z 5P9
Distributed in Great Britain and Europe by Cassell PLC
Villiers House, 41/47 Strand, London WC2N 5JE, England
Distributed in Australia by Capricorn Link (Australia) Pty Ltd.
P.O. Box 6651, Baulkham Hills, Business Centre, NSW 2153, Australia

Printed and bound in Hong Hong

Sterling ISBN 0-8069-0548-4
Front cover photo: *Epiphyllum* hybrid 'Stern von Erlau.'

Contents

Preface

Cacti and other succulents are among the strangest plants on our planet. They have an incomparable wealth of shapes, magnificent blossoms, bizarre spines, and colorful leaves. They awaken in us the desire to collect and to create.

This opulent and colorful guidebook, which is written from the author's personal experience, leads the beginner into the fascinating world of succulents and provides the experienced plant lover with new stimuli. About 140 genera are presented, with extensive information on their care. More than 300 species of succulents, as well as numerous varieties, are included. Basic information about botany and tips on buying, repotting, arranging, grafting, and planting of cacti and other succulents in the garden or in the house round out this guidebook about exotic plants.

Children of the sun: barrel and column cacti and agaves among the annuals.

Interesting Facts About Succulents

Cacti and other succulents are flowering plants. Over a period of many millions of years, they had to adapt themselves to sunny, hot, or dry locations, and therefore they developed highly original shapes. In order to be able to store water for drought periods, they developed succulence or thickness of flesh. To decrease evaporation from surfaces, they developed column- and barrel-shaped forms. For protection against sunlight, they developed rosettes and leaves that are reduced to spines, waxy surfaces, corklike coatings, or silvery hairlike coverings. Let's get to know the native habitats and lives of cacti and other succulents in a brief excursion into botany, and we will immediately understand the requirements of our exotic guests much better.

Aeonium and Opuntia on a rocky slope in the Canary Islands.

Interesting Facts About Cacti

The cactus family is composed of about 100 genera with approximately 2,000 species. Scientists have not agreed on a finalized order in their botanical classification. Although genuine and putative new discoveries become rarer and rarer, they tend to occupy the time of the few experts.

The native habitat of the cacti is (with one exception, namely *Rhipsalis*) the new world, i.e., the Americas from southern Canada to Patagonia. On this north–south expansion of more than 6,200 miles (10,000 km), they can be found in most of the different climate zones. Cacti flourish in rocky areas at heights of 13,000 feet (4,000 m). There the snow piles up, and temperatures can fall far below 0°C (32°F). Cacti grow in massed concentrations in deserts, semideserts, prairies, and dry savannas of the southwest United States, Mexico, and South America, where they have only summer or only winter rains, with two short rain periods in the spring and fall, or only very sporadic, light rainfall. They also live in the foggy deserts on the western slopes of the Andes. Finally, they can even be found in warm, humid tropical and subtropical areas as climbers or epiphytes.

The soil conditions of cacti are just as different as their (always very sparse) water conditions. Desert cacti grow in sand, in volcanic dust, in debris, and in loamy soil, or on mineral soils that are full of nutrition and frequently have high concentrations of salt. Epiphytes grow in the leaf humus of the tropical and subtropical rainforests.

With the exception of the rain forests, native habitats of the cacti have little other vegetation. Plants living in typical cactus habitats have adapted to strong ultraviolet light and to long hours of daily sunshine. They can tolerate high temperatures. In the water-storage tissues of cacti, temperatures of up to about 115°F (45°C) have been measured, while ground temperatures were about 155°F (70°C).

In view of the large variety of cactus habitats, it is not surprising that there is such a variety of genera and species. But it is not necessary to recreate their habitats in order to cultivate cacti. There are very few plants that are more capable of adapting themselves than cacti! *Mammillaria* from Mexico, column cacti from Peru, *Lobivia* from Bolivia, and *Opuntia* from the Rocky Mountains can by all means be kept harmoniously together on a sunny windowsill. Only cacti from dry areas, also known as desert cacti, and those from warm, humid regions have to be taken care of differently.

The Evolution of Cacti

The survival strategies that plants from arid regions (the expert calls these plants *xerophytes*) have come up with

in the course of evolution are as simple as they are efficient. One has to realize that a cactus belongs to the highly developed flowering plants, just as a cyclamen does. Why, then, does it look so different? If you could view evolution occurring, you could observe how a plant that had to survive in a hot, dry place adjusted to its habitat: it shed its leaves completely, or it reduced their size. Either measure would reduce the surface area from which evaporation could take place and protect it from strong sunshine and the heat. Another possibility would be to strengthen its leaf tissue and thus make it resistant to withering. Result: leathery foliage, low on juices. Or the plant might have created a thick exterior tissue of several layers (epidermis) with a strong, waterproof outer coating (cuticle). Sometimes it might include layers of cork or add on colorful wax layers.

How the Shapes of the Cacti Evolved

The ingenious survival techniques of some plants in the hot, dry, gleamingly bright regions led to the typical cactus shape. Cacti reduced the surface area of their bodies. The individual stems become flattened, shaped like columns, bumpy, grooved, or compressed into the shape of a globe or barrel. In the course of evolution, cacti turned their leaves into spines and their branches into *areoles*, localized regions carrying spines and/or bristles. Photosynthesis was taken over mainly by the stems. Bumps (*tubercles*) ribs, warts, hairlike struc-

This is not a photomontage or a picture from another planet. In fact, this gigantic barrel cactus, Ferocactus acanthodes, high above the California coast, is an excellent example of a desert cactus. How much water might it store in its almost 6-foot tall (2 m) body?

Ferocactus acanthodes in its native habitat of California.

tures, and spines provide shade for the plant body and diffuse the light. They also impede evaporation and create condensation points for dew and fog.

The Invention of Succulence

The change to succulence, or thickness of flesh (from the Latin *succus* meaning juice) was certainly the greatest achievement of the cacti. Because of this change, cacti could adapt themselves to a limited water supply, using their slimy, juicy, spongy storage tissue. This tissue is made up of thin-walled cells that (depending on how much water they have) shrivel or become well-rounded. Water-retaining tissues can comprise up to 90% of the plant's volume. These tissues can handle a 60% loss of water without any harm. In almost all cacti, these tissues are located in the stem. The roots, which usually serve for the absorption of water, also store water. That is what the storage roots of *Ariocarpus*, *Coryphantha*, *Dolichothele*, *Gymnocactus*, *Leuchtenbergia*, *Lobivia*, *Mammillaria*, *Neoporteria*, *Oroya*, and especially the large roots of, for example, *Peniocereus* (whose basal stem also stores water) do. Cacti that have tuberous roots use their altered sproutlike roots as storage organs. *Wilcoxia* and *Pterocactus* are thus actually root succulents. Their roots run in general shallowly underneath the soil in order to catch even the slightest amounts of humidity from an area as large as possible. There are also cacti with deep-reaching taproots, which are even capable of tapping into groundwater. However, these often only

Example of an epiphytic cactus, Epiphyllum oxypetalum. This rain-forest cactus from Central and South America has large, sweet-smelling blossoms, with pointed crown leaves. In contrast to desert cacti, epiphytic cacti do not have spines, and their leaves are botanically correct sprouts.

anchor the plant, while the branched-out side roots collect water. In general, cacti create roots easily from the vascular bundles of the central stem. This makes it easy to grow cuttings.

In the formation of a succulent, gas exchange plays a special role. The apertures (stomata) of desert cacti are closed during the day to avoid water loss through evaporation. At night, the carbon dioxide in the air is temporarily bound to malic acid. During the day, when the stomata are closed, these split up again. Only then does normal photosynthesis or assimilation take place.

Blossoms and Fruits

Cactus blossoms are sprout axils of limited growth. As is the case of many plants with two cotyledons, cactus blossoms have shortened, arched, or disk-shaped stems, on which sepals and crown leaves, as well as stamens and fruit leaves, stand vertically or in spirals from the outside to the inside of the stem. If the blossom axil deepens, the way a jug does, and if it finally becomes tube-shaped, the typical cactus blossom is created. In some species, the blossoms develop when the plant is 2 to 3 years old; other plants need to attain a certain height and greater age.

Cactus blossoms are breathtakingly beautiful, but they usually last only one day. Although all colors are represented, blue occurs only in one case—the rare *Wittia amazonica*.

The formation of the blossoms takes place in cacti at the areoles. The blossoms are not protected from transpiration. Therefore, species with large flowers are usually night bloomers. Only

small-blooming species open their blossoms during the day. Many react to light changes and close when it gets cloudy. Day bloomers are usually pollinated in their native habitats by bees, flies, beetles, and birds. In the case of night-blooming cacti, pollination is done by bats and moths. Night bloomers often give off a pleasant scent. Species that are visited by bats can smell sour, musty, or nauseating (to us). The blossoms of *Trixanthocereus* have the worst smell.

When they are ready to blossom, many cacti change their exterior. For example, the *Mammillaria* create white axillary wool. Some grow an entire wool head (cephalium) in clearly set apart flowering areas. A genuine cephalium, a cap-like creation up to 1 yard (1 m) high made of wool hair and bristles, is produced by *Melocactus* and *Discocactus*, but only when the plant is about 10 years old. The growth is considered to be a *pseudocephalium* when the vegetative sprout growth continues out of the hair cap, as for example in the case of *Morawetzia* or *Arrojadoa*. The so-called *lateral cephalium* grows vertically at the sprout on one side. It can be found in a number of *Cereus*. Almost all cacti are dependent on pollination by others, i.e., animals like insects, birds, or bats. Only in *Frailea*, *Melocactus*, and *Rhipsalis* does self-pollination take place.

After pollination and fertilization, the ovary of some species, including certain *Mammillaria* and the *Hamatocactus*, turns into a strikingly red or yellow

Epiphyllum oxypetalum in its native habitat of Guatemala.

berry, which contains the seeds. Seeds are an important criterion for the systematic categorization of species.

Cacti of Humid, Warm Areas

Cacti of these areas are the outsiders of the family. All they have in common with the succulent desert cacti is the reduction of their leaves. The exceptions, the *Pereskia*, has deciduous leaves. The sprouts are flattened and thin, but they don't have the transpiration-protection measures of other cacti, although they take over the leaf functions.

Leaf cacti are an example. Cacti in this environment strive for light in the dusky jungle. They live as climbers (*Hylocereus, Selenicereus, Pereskia,* and *Epiphyllum*). They sit in the forks of rainforest giants or on exposed, naked rocks, without connection to the soil, as epiphytes (*Aporocactus, Rhipsalis,* and *Schlumbergera*). Epiphytic cacti of the species *Rhipsalis* are found in Africa, on Madagascar, Zanzibar, and in Ceylon, by the way.

History of the Cacti

The oldest fossil cactus remains date from the Eocene, about 50 million years ago, in Utah and Colorado. The Aztec priests in Mexico used large, globe-shaped specimens of *Echinocactus ingens* and *E. grandis* as sacrificial tables to cut out the hearts of their sacrifices in honor of the god of war. During cult ceremonies, the Indians ate parts of the peyote cactus, *Lophophora williamsii*, which contains 15 hallucinogenic alkaloids, of which mescaline, which is related to LSD, is the most important one.

Presumably, cacti came to Europe by way of the conquerors of the new world. In the 16th century, they were mentioned for the first time in herb books. By the 17th century, genera were already being distinguished, including *Cereus, Pereskia,* and *Opuntia*. In 1737, Linnaeus, the great botanist, combined the 24 known species into one genus, *Cactus*. The word itself originates from Greek and means "the bristly plant." At first, only the aristocracy got excited about cacti. Later, the middle class also became interested. In 1892 the German Cactus Society was founded. After World War I and again after World War II, downright cacti "booms" occurred, resulting in irresponsible pillage in the native countries of the cacti. Fortunately, cacti were included in the International Species Protection Regulations agreed upon in Washington in 1973. Today, every cactus lover can get unusual species of cacti from the enormous supply of horticultural plants.

Products from Cacti

Noteworthy economic uses of cacti barely exist. Some cacti have edible fruit, like *Opuntia ficus-indica*. In Mexico, peeled pieces of *Echinocactus* are cut into small pieces, candied, and sold as "candy cactus." Many column *Cereus* provide fruit, which are available as pitayas in delicatessen stores and markets. *Opuntia* also played a role as host-plant of the cochineal louse, which provided a scarlet-red dye that was formerly used in the cosmetics industry; today it has been replaced by aniline dyes.

Groups for Cactus Lovers

It is well known that shared fun is double fun. Everywhere in Europe and the United States, there are cactus lovers who have united in order to share information. The activities of these groups include workshops, slide shows, exchange programs, trips to purchase plants, descriptions of newly discovered species, journals, collection of funds, and running their own libraries. Their goals are the exchange of scientific research, conveying knowledge of botany, sharing information about the growth and care of cacti, and the protection of nature and of the world of plants.

Protection of Species

For a long time, imported plants from the origin countries were collector's items, especially high in demand. As a result, too many species were almost made extinct in their native lands. Since 1973, the trade in endangered plants, their parts, and products has been strictly supervised according to the so-called Washington Agreement to Protect Species. Imports and purchases are regulated, restricted, or forbidden. The following cactus genera are affected at this time by the agreement: *Ariocarpus, Astrophytum, Aztekium, Backebergia, Coryphantha, Echinocereus, Echinomastus, Leuchtenbergia, Mammillaria, Pediocactus, Pelecyphora, Sclerocactus, Turbinicarpus,* and *Wilcoxia*.

Fascinating bristly varieties of cactus.

Uebelmannia pectinifera

Browningia hertlingiana

Denmoza erythrocephala

Echinofossulocactus pentacanthus

Echinocactus ingens

Opuntia microdasys

Carnegia gigantea

Cephalocereus senilis

The shape, arrangement, length, strength, and color of spines vary widely in cacti. They depend on the species and variety, but they can also be influenced by environmental conditions. However, the arrangement of areoles remains the same and is thus a reliable feature for botanical classification. To the left are cacti with typical spines: Uebelmannia pectinifera with comb-like prickles. Browningia hertlingiana in its youth, with a few yellow-brown spines. Denmoza erythrocephala, with fox-red spines and white bristle hairs. Echinofossulocactus pentacanthus, with mostly upward-bent spines. Echinocactus ingens, with coarse, densely standing spines. Carnegia gigantea, with yellowish spines that may be 2½ inches (7 cm) long. Opuntia microdasys, with typical bundled, white glochids (bristles). Cephalocereus senilis, with a coat of long white bristle hairs.

The Fascinating Variety of Shapes

Cacti are among the most bizarre of the flora; they produce magnificent blossoms in wonderful colors. The unusual shapes, decorative spines, and ridges of the cacti are just as admirable as the shapes of roses and cyclamen, which also are flowering plants. The wide range of shape transformations of cacti may be seen in morphological oddities like rock-shaped or fan-shaped cacti.

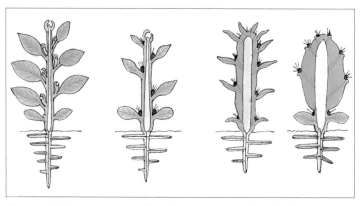

Plant evolution: From a herblike plant a cactus evolves. 1: Flowering plant with sprout, leaves, and axillary buds. 2: The axillary buds are transformed into short young spined shoots (areoles); the leaves become spines. 3 and 4: The upper leaves become more and more reduced in size; the sprout shaft slowly becomes succulent.

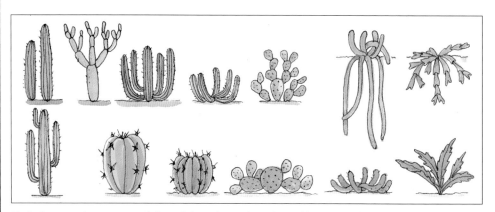

Typical cactus shapes. From left to right: column-shaped; treelike growth; basally branched columns; shrublike growth; hanging growth; hanging leaf shoots; candelabrum shape; thick-columned; short, cylindrical growth; globular; bumpy growth; cushion-shaped; low-lying with upright leaf shoots.

Roots and Sprouts

Cacti have several different types of root system. Most have shallow roots. These enable them to take advantage of the short rainstorms that occur in their habitats. There are also species with water-storing roots. Epiphytic cacti have adhesive roots. Climbing cacti have clinging shoots with roots that spring up on them, or hook-like barbs, which support them as they climb.

The body of the cactus was created through adaptation to an extremely dry location (see illustrations at left). The spines (or thorns as they are called in common everyday language, even though this is not botanically correct) are leaves of the cactus that have been reduced to a minimum. They sit on the areoles. On the outside are edge spines, which can be all of the same shape or of different length and color. In contrast to them, the mostly strong, often hooklike, bent, twisted, ringletlike, or flattened central spines stand out.

Shapes

Cacti grow in many different shapes. Treelike species can grow 40 to 50 feet (12 to 15 m) tall; for example, *Platyopuntia* or *Browningia* species, *Pachycereus pringlei*, or *Carnegia gigantea*. Column cacti may have single or branched shapes. Certain *Cephalocereus* and *Neobuxbaumia* species have only a single shaft. Much more often, side branches are created, as for example in *Haageocereus, Espostoa, Eulychnia*. Branches growing close to the ground become sparlike shrubs. If the sprouts lie on the ground, roots on the sprouts are created, and a kind of cushion arises, as for example with many *Mammillaria*, *Ferocactus*, *Tephrocactus*, and *Echinocereus* species.

The globe or barrel shape, more or less distinct, ranging from plate-flat to thick, columnlike ones, is the most common cactus shape.

Climbing forms have long limbs. They branch out in a shrublike fashion; for example, *Selenicereus* or *Hylocereus*.

Hanging forms can be found in many epiphytic species, such as *Nopalxochia* and *Schlumbergera*, but also in *Aporocactus* and *Hildewintera*.

Special Features

Cristate form, growth that is fasciated or fanlike, is created randomly at the growth tip. The sprout axil widens like a band, and helmet- or cockscomb-shaped deformities are created. Cristate forms can disappear totally or partially, and they are not hereditary. They do not always flower, but when they do, the flowers are abundant.

Monstrous forms arise genetically; they are hereditary deformities. They have irregularly arranged and running ribs, which bent. The side branches are hardly developed, or they have grown into each other. In the same way, areoles melt together, leading to bizarre rocklike creations.

Blossom and pollinator go together.

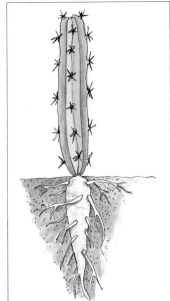

Tuberous roots *store water in some cacti.*

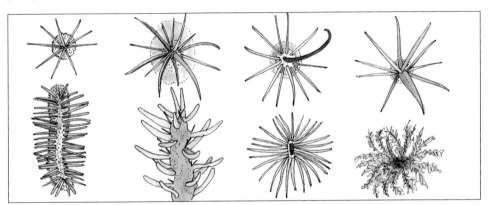

Various spine configurations. *Spines can be arranged in the shape of a star, a wreath, or a comb. On the outer edges are the edge spines; they all may be formed the same way or may differ in length, thickness, and color. The middle or central spines distinguish themselves from these. They are usually stronger, often hooklike, bent, twisted, ringlet-like, flattened, or striking in some other way.*

Monstrous forms *are deformities in which side branches grow together, with melted-together areoles and bent ribs.*

Cockscomb shapes. *Growth deficiencies at the tip of the sprout lead to deformities that resemble a cockscomb.*

Interesting Facts About Other Succulents

All cacti belong to the Cactaceae family. Other succulents exist in about 50 different plant families, with more than 600 genera and thousands of species. Like cacti, succulents also inhabit arid areas, although succulents live in other climates, too. Different amounts of rainfall, divergent temperatures, and variable wind and light conditions influence the life cycles of succulents. Most of the approximately 3000 succulent species inhabit the sunniest areas of the earth, especially in Africa: the Cape region and the Karoo (South Africa); Namaqualand (South Africa and Namibia); the Namib Desert, the dry areas of East Africa, and the southern part of Morocco, as well as the islands of Madagascar and Socotra. Regarding Asia, there are only a couple of *Euphorbia* and *Stapelia* in India. Although the huge deserts of Australia have xerophytes (plants that have adapted themselves to dry conditions), they basically have no succulents. In the Americas, leaf succulents, such as agave, Crassulaceae (including sedum and *Echeveria*), and *Pachypodium* grow; stem succulents like *Euphorbia* are unusual. In Europe (except for the Canary Islands), there are only alien plants like agave and *Opuntia*, which particularly live in the Mediterranean area, and some sedum and *Sempervivum* species. Worldwide (except for some polar

areas) only *Crassula* species and *Cissus quadrangularis* are widespread. There also are succulent inhabitants of warm, humid tropical zones, for example aloe species, ephiphytes, Peruvian *Peperomia* species, and climbing plants, such as *Hoya* from southeast Asia and Australia.

Appearance and Survival Strategies

Although many succulents look like cacti, there are fundamental differences. The spines of cacti are transformed leaves. On the other hand, the thorns of *Euphorbia*, which are similar in their habitus, are completely or partially transformed side branches, or, as in the case of the *Senecio* and *Crassula* species, they are transformed inflorescences. Real spines that are not ligneous (woody), pointy outgrowths of the surface tissue are the leaf spines of some agaves and aloes, as well as those of *Euphorbia milii*, or crown-of-thorns.

Leaf Succulents

The structure of most cacti appears to be rather uniform; the variety of shapes of the other succulents is incredibly large, however. The essential morphological characteristics of succulents have already been addressed in the chapter on cacti as prototypes of the succulent plants. The attempt to keep the surface area as small as possible (the smaller, the drier), to protect against too

much water evaporation, frequently concerns the leaves in the case of succulents, for example the aloe, *Lithops*, and Crassulaceae. They are often shaped like cylinders or globes, as in the case of *Conophytum*. The leaves may be shaped like scales and lie densely around the stem as in *Senecio*, or they may overlap each other, arranged as dense rosettes, as in *Echeveria*. Rosette leaves can spread themselves out like a funnel and can catch water. When they are dry, the leaves curve inwards, so that evaporation is decreased.

In some species, the small, thick leaves lie so densely and crosswise on top of each other around the sprout axis that only their edges have stomata and chloroplasts, and take over transpiration, oxygen exchange, and photosynthesis, as for example, in *Crassula pyramidalis*. Two rows of alternately standing leaves can be found on *Gasteria*. The rows stand opposite each other in pairs on *Crassula arborescens*.

During dry periods, many succulents shed their foliage or drastically diminish the number of their leaves. Minimally, only one pair is formed, which, in addition, grows together, except for a gap. During the dry period, it shrivels to a paperlike wrapper, underneath which the new leaf pair develops.

The construction of the leaves serves the purpose of giving up less water to the outside. Many leaves have a strong, thick epidermis, and they are often densely covered with hair or wax, as well as being equipped with narrow, clogged, sunken,

Aeonium subplanum in its natural habitat. It is clearly evident how the succulent curves its rosette leaves inwards, in order to decrease the evaporation surfaces exposed to the sun.

Aeonium subplanum in its native habitat.

overlapped (wind-protected) apertures (stomata) on the top and bottom.

There are also ingenious devices that serve for the absorption of water: leaf hair, as in the case of *Crassula* species, *Trichodiadema*, and others; specially elastic epidermis cells, which swell and shrivel again, as in *Adromischus* and *Kalanchoe*; and air roots and side leaves, which can absorb humidity, as in the case of the *Anacampseros* species.

The *Lithops* are especially strange. On their highly succulent, frequently club-shaped leaves, the central water storage tissue at the end reaches up to below the epidermis, which is completely or partially free of chloroplasts. The leaf end, therefore, seems to be transparent, like a window. The rest of the plant body is buried in the ground. Sunlight, although necessary for photosynthesis, is often too intense. It reaches the chloroplast layers, which are protected, very slowly through the "window." Small spots on the surface, which sometimes flow together as in marble, create patterns that serve as camouflage for the plants among the stones (mimesis is another adaptation).

Stem and Root Succulents

Not all succulents are leaf succulents. *Euphorbia*, with their green rinds, and *Stapelia* have no leaves at all, or only rudimentary leaves. In their stead, the stem, with a decreased surface area, stores water, either throughout or only at the bulblike, thickened base. The stem performs the functions of photosynthesis and transpiration. It develops the usual protective devices against water shortage: a corklike coat, wax layers, and stabilizing enforcement tissue (this happens, for example, in *Kalanchoë* and aloe). Such plants are stem succulents and, at the same time, are convergent with many cacti. Examples of stem succulents are: *Euphorbia*, *Stapelia*, *Huernia*, and *Kleinia*, in which the entire stem or only the thickened stem base serves for water storage. A few species are also root succulents. Their plant parts above ground hardly seem to be succulent.

Blossoms, Fruit and Seeds

The blossoms of succulents are, depending on their family affiliation, quite varied. The blossom colors range from white and yellow to red in all shades. Blue blossoms only occur in *Sedum caeruleum*.

These fully grown specimens of the Madagascar palm tree can be admired in the Grigsby Gardens in California. The white blossoms clearly show the affiliation to the Apocynaceae (dogbane) family. The Madagascar palm tree (Pachypodium lamerei) needs to attain a certain age in order to blossom for the first time; in a pot one can count on it, as a rule of thumb, when it has reached a height of 47 inches (120 cm)

Botanical Families With Prominent Succulent Representatives		
Family	Genus	Well-Known Species
Agavaceae (Agave plants)	Agave Sansevieria	A. victoria-reginae Mother-in law's tongue
Aizoaceae (Mesembryanthemaceae)	Argyroderma Cephalophyllum Conophytum Faucaria Fenestraria Frithia Gibbaeum Glottiphyllum Lithops Oophytum Ophthalmophyllum Pleiospilos Rhombophyllum Ruschia Schwantesia Titanopsis Trichodiadema	Tiger's jaws Window plant Tongueleaf Living stones
Apocynaceae (Dogbane)	Adenium Pachypodium Plumeria	Desert rose Madagascar palm tree Frangipani
Asclepiadaceae (milkweed family)	Caralluma Ceropegia Duvalia Hoodia Hoya Huernia Stapelia Trichocaulon	Wax flower Carrion plant
Commelinaceae	Tradescantia	Spiderwort
Compositae	Senecio	Cineraria
Crassulaceae	Adromischus Aeonium Cotyledon Crassula Echeveria Dudleya Graptopetalum Kalanchoe Sedum Sempervivum	Plover eggs Velvet rose Botterboom Jade tree Mexican firecracker Velvet leaf Hens and chicks Houseleek
Euphorbiaceae	Euphorbia Monadenium Pedilanthus Synadenium	Crown-of-thorns Living baseball Poinsettia Pachysandra African milk bush
Geraniaceae (storksbill)	Pelargonium	Geranium
Liliceae	Aloe Gasteria Haworthia	Medicinal aloe Cow-tongue cactus Star cactus
Portulacaceae	Anacampseros Portulacaria	Love plant Portulaca

Madagascar palm tree.

Some succulents flower once a year, for example, *Portulaca* and *Dorotheanthus*. Others bloom twice a year. Agaves flower only after 7 to 10 years; then they die, but they reproduce beforehand. Although small blossoms use much less water than large ones, even small ones only open for a short time.

The blossoms of the *Stapelia* are fleshy and stay open for a couple of days. Self-pollination rarely occurs. Extreme cross-pollination occurs in dioecious plants, for example, *Euphorbia obesa* and *Dioscorea elephantipes* (syn. *Testudinaria*). The seed pods contain seeds that range in size from very small to pea-sized. The berries of *Cissus* and *Cyphostemma* are fleshy fruits. Crassulaceae, Asclepiadaceae, and Apocynaceae have dry fruit (from a fruit-leaf) with bursting belly seams; lily and agave plants have a capsule of at least two fruit leaves; Euphorbiaceae have dehiscent fruit.

Seeds are dispersed by wind, water, animals, and human beings. Some succulents, for example, *Crassula sarmentosa*, propagate through shoots; others, such as *Kalanchoe*, through leaves or plantlets.

Products from Succulents

Some succulents are of economic importance in their native lands. Numerous agave live in tropical and subtropical regions, particularly in Central America, and are important plants there, cultivated in fields. Mexicans drink the fresh juice of several agaves as *aguamiel* or their fermented juice as *pulque*, the Mexican national beverage, or distilled as *tequila*.

Agave sisalina is a productive fibrous plant. It is planted in the tropics all over the world, mostly on large plantations, for the production of sisal. The sisal agave lives 6–12 years; during this time it creates a rosette tree, up to 3 feet (1 m) high, which is crowned by the leaf rosette. In the vegetative phase, 15 to 20 leaves spring up every year. They are cut after 2 to 4 years. A machine removes the fibres from the fleshy leaves while they are still fresh. The fibre is collected in bundles 3 to 6 feet (1 to 2 m) long. After being washed and dried, the shiny yellow fibres become soft again through beating and brushing. Thread, rope, nets, hammocks, furniture materials, and carpets are made from sisal fibre. The leaf fibres of the Mexican *henequen*, *Agave fourcroydes*, are utilized in the same way. The fibres of the bow hemp, a *Sansevieria*, are also useful.

The aloe is among the oldest medicinal remedies and cosmetics. Nefertiti and Cleopatra used the juice of the succulent lily plant as a complexion aid. For the Indians, the aloe was "magic from heaven." The Chinese use it even today as a medicinal and beauty device. In Europe, aloe has been known for 150 years. Particularly in the country, everyone kept a fire aloe (*Aloe arborescens*) as a first aid plant in a pot or bucket. Burns and scraped knees of children were successfully treated with the cooling and healing juice of the plant. For cosmetic purposes especially, *Aloe vera* (syn. *Aloe barbadensis*) is planted today on plantations. It grows taller than a yard (1 m), with leaves in rosette form. The leaves, about 32 inches (80 cm) long, can become 1 inch (3 cm) thick and often weigh more than 2 lbs (1 kg). In order to get the valuable aloe gel, the leaf epidermis is peeled by hand off the colorless, slimy, inner parenchyma. It can be applied fresh to the skin or can be made into a gel, used in cosmetics.

Several aloe species are used in the pharmaceutical industry. Thus, the thickened leaf-juice of the *Aloe ferox* serves as a laxative in cases of chronic constipation. Effective ingredients are aloin, resins and bitter principles. Aloe powder, cooked in water (about 1 knife-tip in about ¼ litre [8 oz.] of water) was formerly used as an eyewash in cases of cloudy or infected eyes and also to heal wounds that did not want to heal.

The fragrant frangipani (*Plumeria rubra* and *P. alba*) is another succulent with a historic background. It was discovered by botanist Mercutio Frangipani at the end of the 15th century. It owes its botanical name, *Plumeria*, to the discoverer Charles Plumier (1646–1706). The origin of its common name is uncertain. Was is called after its discoverer or, because its blossoms smelled just as wonderful, after a perfume that already had existed 300 years earlier and bore the same name, which the Italian perfume-mixer Frangipani had mixed out of different essential oils? This perfume, favorite scent of the legendary Catherine de Medici, was throughout decades the favorite scent of high society and remained famous for a long time.

The photo on page 23 shows Opuntia, different agaves, crown-of-thorn plants, and summer annuals, planted directly in the soil. While Opuntia in favorable locations can survive the winter outside, agaves and crown-of-thorns have to be brought inside before the first frost. It is therefore recommended that when they are planted outside, they be lowered into the ground in their pots.

Opuntia, agave, Euphorbia, and various summer annuals planted outside.

Plant and Blossom Shapes of Other Succulents

Although the variety of the cacti is impressive, one is even more astonished, when looking at the other succulents, at the never-ending creativity of nature. Some of these blossoms look like art-deco chandeliers or jewelry. Designers can still learn something from the beauty and perfection of the leaf rosettes of the succulents.

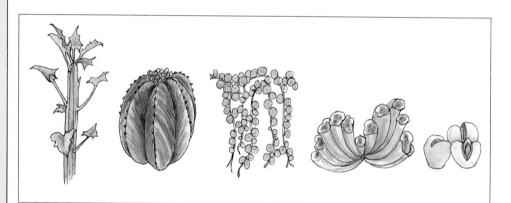

Plant shapes, 1. *From left to right: Succulent shoot of Senecio articulatus from the Compositae family; globe-shaped Euphorbia obesa; "strings of pearls" of Senecio rowleyanus, also from the Compositae family; fan with two parts of Haworthia truncata, a lily plant, and a globular Conophytum species from the Aizoaceae family.*

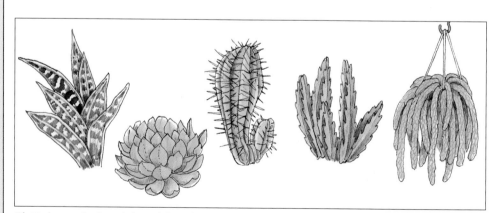

Plant shapes, 2. *From left to right: Aloe variegata, a lily plant with leaves standing like over-lapped roof tiles; rosette of Echeveria from the Crassulaceae family; the columnlike shape of Euphorbia horrida (Euphorbiacea family); little stems with four sides on Stapelia hirsuta (Asclepiadaceae family); and sausage-shaped branches of Sedum morganianum (Crassulaceae family).*

Plant Shapes

Succulents have an immense variety of shapes. In addition to globes and columns, the rosettes have numerous variations, for example, in *Haworthia*, *Aeonium*, and *Echeveria*. The "strings of pearls" of some *Senecio* species and the strange "pebbles" of the "window-leaf plants"—for example, *Lithops* and *Conophytum*—look bizarre as well.

Blossom Shapes

The blossom shapes are even more varied than the plant shapes of the succulents.

Crassula blossoms are simple. They are small and upright. From the outside to the inside, the whorls of the sepals, crown leaves, stamens, and fruit leaves spread out like stars. Most of the blossoms are whitish or reddish.

Stapelia blossoms are unusually shaped and colored. They smell like a carcass. The "star" of a *Stapelia* blossom is equipped with a small, insignificant calyx with five crown tips (which grow together at the bottom into a tube), and a ring around the actual sex organs. Within the ring, five stamens, which are raised and which enclose two free fruit leaves, are surrounded by an outer and an inner side crown. On the bottom the sepals are grayish or reddish; on the upper side, they are callous, grooved, or hairy, and very strikingly brown or violet in color.

Euphorbia have hermaphroditic flowers, in which a female blossom is surrounded by five groups of male blossoms. In order to avoid self-pollination, the female stigma ripens before the male stamens. In many *Euphorbia*, the cyathia (inflorescences) are of one gender. On one plant there are either male or female flowers, but the flowers are always rather simple ones.

Ceropegia blossoms are ingenious traps for small fruit flies. The flies fall through the five slots of the umbrella-shaped tip into the tube. Since the way out is blocked, the insects have to pollinate the plant. After pollination has occurred, the flower fades, the smooth inside walls of the calyx become wrinkled, the hair becomes limp and thus the way out is opened up.

In *Senecio* species, the blossoms sit together to create little baskets. The individual blossom is usually a so-called disk blossom, which is tube-shaped with a five-lobed corolla.

Convergence

When plants of totally different origins on two separate continents, such as America and Africa, under the same climate conditions choose the same shape or form (for example, the cactus form), it is called *convergence*. In the case of the cacti of the new world and the *Euphorbia* of the old world, this happens frequently. Well-known species pairs are: *Euphorbia obesa* and *Astrophytum asterias*; *Euphorbia horrida* and *Lobivia ferox*; and *Stapelia grandiflora*, *Senecio stapeliiformis* and *Cissus quadrangularis*.

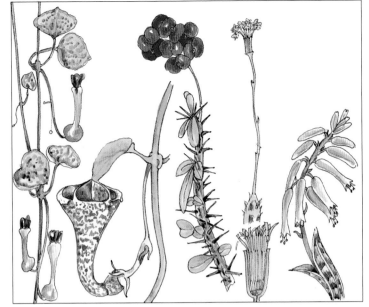

Blossom shapes, 1. *From left to right: Ceropegia woodii, C. distincta ssp. haygarthii, Euphorbia milii, Senecio, Aloe.*

Blossom shapes, 2. *From left to right: Adenium obesum (top), Titanopsis calcarea, Echeveria, Stapelia variegata, Graptopetalum bellum.*

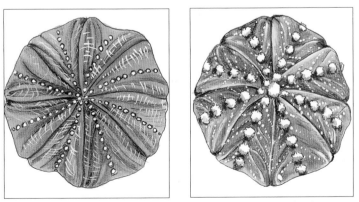

Example of convergence. *At left, Euphorbia obesa from South Africa. At right, the cactus Astrophytum asterias from Mexico. Notice the amazing similarity of shape and the remarkable symmetry of these two plants.*

A Short Succulents Dictionary

To describe cacti and other succulents, there are a number of scientific terms that can't easily be replaced with ordinary words, so when you come to one in the text, have a quick look here whenever you do not understand a botanical or horticultural term.

Air roots: Organs of tropical plants that absorb air, water, and nutrients. Air roots can branch out if they come into contact with the soil and can serve as support for the plant.

Annulus: Ring-shaped outgrowth of the corolla in some *Stapelia*.

Areoles: The spiny cushions of cactus.

Axil: The distal angle of divergence between a branch or a leaf and the axis from which it arises.

Bastard: A hybrid of inferior quality, the product of chance interbreeding.

Bristle tufts of hair: Preliminary stage of a cephalium.

Callus: Corklike tissue, which develops from the phloem or cortex over any cut or wounded surface of stem or root.

Calyx: All the sepals together constitute the calyx.

Caudex: an enlarged storage organ at soil level, it may be a swollen stem, a root, or both.

Cephalium: Bristly and hairy tufts arising in the flowering zone, out of which, in the case of some cacti, the flowers grow.

Cleistogamous: Capable of setting viable seed without the flowers opening.

Convergence: A similarity of shape and appearance occurring in unrelated plants.

Corolla: All the petals together constitute the corolla.

Cristate shapes: Cockscomb or fasciashaped growth deformities of branches or stems.

Cultivar: A plant form that originates in cultivation.

Cuticle: Waxlike, water-resistant, transpiration-preventing, and ultraviolet-radiation-repelling skin layer above the epidermis of the plant.

Cyathium: The tiny, reduced inflorescence of the Euphorbiaceae.

Epidermis: Layers that make up the outer covering of a plant.

Epiphytes, epiphytic plants: Plants that in their natural location do not grow in the earth, but in the branched forks of trees, and which are not parasites.

Evolution: The biogenetic and phylogenetic development of plants or animals.

Family: A taxonomic grouping of genera with shared characteristics. Family names usually end in—aceae.

Fasciation: Malformation of plant stems resulting from more or less disorganized tissue growth.

Genus: A taxonomic group of related species (sometimes containing one species only).

Glochidia (glochids): Tiny single-celled bristle hairs, equipped with barbs, found on the *Opuntia*.

Guard cells: Two cells on the sides of each stoma that contain chlorophyll; they can close up to close the stoma, or open to create a connection between the exterior air and the air inside the plant.

Habitus: Exterior shape of a plant; form.

Hermaphroditic blossoms: Bisexual blossoms that contain both the male and female organs, stamen and pistil.

Honey glands: Blossom organs of the *Euphorbiaceae*, which lure insects with a honeylike secretion.

Hybrid: Cross-product of plants of different genera, species, or varieties.

Inflorescence: The mode of development and arrangement of flowers on an axis.

Lamellar: Having a shape composed of thin plates.

Lateral cephalium: A lateral or one-sided cephalium.

Latex: In succulents, a white milky fluid, typically found in Euphor-

biaceae and some Asclepiadaceae; it is sometimes very poisonous.

Mimesis: Adaptation of the plant's exterior by imitating its environment in coloration or shape.

Monstrous forms: Inherited growth anomalies.

Mutation: A genetic change that occurs either spontaneously or is caused artificially, for example through use of chemicals or radiation, and which can be inherited.

Offset: A smaller plant or shoot arising from the base of the parent plant, which, when separated, can easily grow roots and develop further.

Pectinate: Comblike growth form.

Petals: The inner circle of flower leaves that comprise the corolla of a flower.

Photoperiodicity: The reaction of a plant to the length of the light and dark periods of a day.

Photosynthesis: The process by which green plants change carbon dioxide from the air and hydrogen from water into glucose, by means of chlorophyll-containing cells exposed to sunlight. During photosynthesis, oxygen is released.

Phylloclade: A flattened stem or branch that functions as a leaf.

Pistil: The ovule-bearing (female) organ of a plant, including the ovary, style, and stigma.

Prickle: A small spine or thorn.

Pseudocephalium: A false cephalium, which sometimes is perfoliated by sprouts.

Respiration: The life process of releasing the potential energy of food in a usable form by oxidation.

Ribs: Raised ridges that form on the epidermis of some plants.

Root succulents: Plants whose roots store water.

Rosette: A dense arrangement of leaves on an extremely shortened sprout axil.

Sepals: The protective flower leaves that form an outer circle at the flower base and protect the flower when it is a bud. All the sepals together constitute the calyx.

Side sprout: Sprout that can be separated from the parent plant and that then will grow roots.

Spines: Bristles, stickers, or prickles created by the metamorphosis of leaves, sprouts, or roots.

Stamen: The male organ of the flower, whose knoblike top (anther) produces pollen.

Stem succulents: Plants in which the stem contains water-storing tissue.

Stigma: The expanded sticky top of the pistil, which receives the pollen.

Stoma (pl., stomata): A breathing-pore in the lower epidermis of leaves or stems through which gaseous interchange between the atmosphere and the intercellular spaces of leaves and stems can occur.

Style: The elongated portion of a pistil that connects the ovary with the stigma of a plant.

Taxonomy: The science of classification of organisms into order, family, genus, and species.

Thorns: Short, rigid, sharp-pointed leafless branches.

Transpiration: The process by which a plant gives off water vapor.

Tubercle: A knoblike growth on a stem or leaf.

Window leaves: Fleshy leaves that have transparent zones that are low on chlorophyll, but admit light, as in *Lithops*.

Zygomorphic blossoms: Blossoms that are capable of being divided symmetrically in one plane only, the two halves being mirror images of each other, for example, *Schlumbergera*, *Cleistocactus*, *Denmoza*, and *Matucana*.

Guide to the Alphabetical Listings

On the following 93 pages, you will get to know the most beautiful succulent plants for cultivation in and around the house. The alphabetical part is divided into two lists. At first, the best-known cacti are introduced, which all belong to the Cactaceae family (pp. 30–83). After that, a second list of other succulents follows; they belong to many different plant families (pp. 85–121). The plant descriptions are arranged as follows:

Botanical Name: The botanical name is valid internationally, so it is mentioned first and it determines the alphabetical order. If a genus is discussed, only the genus name is listed, for example *Mammillaria*. If only one species is discussed, for example, *Aztekium ritteri*, the species name *ritteri* is listed as well. Additional genera, which at this time are classified under the genus that is being discussed, are listed as well.

Common name: Where there is a well-known common name, it is listed, somewhat smaller, below the botanical name.

Photographs: Each genus or species is pictured; often there are also several species or variations.

Symbols: These show you at one glance the important characteristics, features, and requirements of the plant. Asterisk (*) indicates the winter rest period temperature.

○	Globe-shaped	▮ About 32°–46°F (0°–8°C)*	
▯	Column-shaped	▮ About 46°–54°F (8°–12°C)*	
⌇	Climbing plant	▮ More than 54°F (12°C)*	
⌇	Hanging plant		
⌇	Creeping plant	🪣 Soil rich in humus	
🌼	Cushion-shaped	🪣 Soil rich in minerals	
🌼	Rosette		
🌿	Stinky blossoms	💧 High demand for water	
🌿	Pleasant-smelling blossoms	💧 Medium demand for water	
		💧 Little demand for water	
○	Light		
☼	Full sun	▲ High demand for nutrients	
◐	Half shade	▲ Medium demand for nutrients	
●	Shaded	△ Little demand for nutrients	
		☒ Poisonous plant	

General notes: Contains plant descriptions and information about their natural habitats.

Care: Gives the most important tips for year-round care.

Species: Here you will find brief information about species (or variations) that are worth cultivating and are well known; most have a description of the blossom color, important for the purchase. Plants that were deliberately bred receive a cv. (cultivar); the cultivar epithet is put into quotation marks, hybrids are marked with an × in front of them. Mutations or other striking biotypes are classified under f. for form.

Extra tip: Here you will find important hints for care, or other information that is worthwhile stressing.

The Most Beautiful Cacti and Their Care

Few indoor plants produce such magnificent blossoms as this leaf cactus, *Epiphyllum* 'Demetrius.' When you learn in addition that such a plant can be extremely easy to care for, you soon will be grabbed by cactus fever.

Cactus blossoms are something special for flower lovers. The blossoms are anticipated with pleasure, and they can be achieved with little expertise. People who work with the prickly creatures discover the never-ending wealth of ideas in nature: cacti as shrubs or trees, globes and columns, dwarfs and giants. There are naked ones and those with tufts of hair. Their spines are always different: long and short, thick and needlelike, straight and crooked, one-colored and patterned, smooth and rough—each kind a small wonder in itself.

A splendid leaf cactus, Epiphyllum hybrid 'Demetrius.'

Acanthocalycium

Acanthorhipsalis

Ancistrocactus

Acanthocalycium violaceum originates in northern Argentina and has distinctive long spines and numerous blossoms. The cactus needs a specially sunny location.

Acanthorhipsalis monacantha is especially pretty when adorned by pinkish carmine-colored fruit, which are in any case more attractive than the rather plain blossoms.

The greenish yellow-brown blossoms of Ancistrocactus scheeri stand out very little, although they grow most of the time in multiples.

Acanthocalycium violaceum.

Acanthorhipsalis monacantha.

Ancistrocactus scheeri.

General notes: Acanthocalycium species grow in northern Argentina at heights of up to 3250 feet (1000 m). The plant body is short and cylindrical with ribs that have dense spines; it can grow up to 8 inches (20 cm) tall. From May or June on, it carries large, funnel-shaped, white, yellow, or reddish blossoms close to the crown, which remain open for several days.
Care: Easy. The plants need a sunny to partially shady, not very hot location and a nutritious, slightly acidic soil. Do not keep them too wet in the summer, and keep them dry during the winter rest period at 46° to 50°F (8° to 10°C). Propagate by seed.
Species: *A. glaucum*, blue-green with black spines and 2¼-inch-long (6 cm) yellow blossoms.
  A. violaceum, matte light green with up to 1⅛-inch-long (3 cm) straight yellowish spines. Many pale lilac-colored blossoms, which grow up to 3 inches (7.5 cm) long.

General notes: This genus is classified today under *Rhipsalis*. It includes epiphytic, strongly branched, mostly hanging plants, which grow in Peru, Bolivia, and Argentina. In contrast to *Rhipsalis*, it has areoles that are clearly covered with spines. The blossoms are small and white, orange, or red.
Care: An airy location out of the sun that is warm, always moderately moist, without dryness for the roots in the summer and with a temperature above 54°F (12°C) in the winter is most suitable for these plants. Also recommended are frequent fogging, an acidic, peat-containing, porous soil with a perlite portion, and fertilizing in small dosages, with emphasis on nitrogen.
Species: *A. crenata*, bushy with roundly arched shoots and red blossoms.
  A. incahuasia and *A. micrantha* with purple blossoms, *A. monacantha* with orange-colored blossoms, *A. paranganiensis*, with cream-white blossoms.

General notes: The native habitats of this genus are Mexico and Texas, USA. Spines of different colors sit on globular bodies with ribs that are strongly tubercled. The middle spines always have hooks; the blossoms are small and cream-colored, greenish, pink, or lemon-yellow; the seeds are blackish brown.
Care: Difficult. Sunny location, porous soil mixed with sand. Do not keep too moist. Grafting is absolutely necessary.
Species: *A. brevihamatus*, up to 4 inches (10 cm) tall, has white edge needles and black middle needles, with pink blossoms.
  A. megarhizus, spiral ribs, blossoms greenish yellow.
  A. scheeri, globular or club-shaped body, edge needles white to yellow, middle needles black-, brown- and white-speckled; blossoms greenish to brownish.
  A. tobuschii. The plant body, sitting partially in the ground, is blue-green. Edge needles are white, middle needles are yellow; blossoms are whitish to lemon yellow.

Aporocactus

Aporocactus flagelliformis.

General notes: These Mexican epiphytic cacti are especially suitable for hanging plants because of the way they grow. The genus name is derived from the Greek word *aporos* = entangled + *kaktos* = prickly plant.

Care: Easy. Beginners have luck with these robust cacti. *Aporocactus* wants a bright to sunny location; in the summer in a protected spot outside in the full sun. The soil should be nutritious and slightly acidic, the water soft or softened. Water the plants frequently in the summer; in the winter keep only moist. They do not tolerate the wet soil that results from poor drainage. The older the plant gets, the more abundantly one has to fertilize. In the winter, keep them in a bright and not too cool location. Propagate through cuttings; older plants do not tolerate repotting very well.

Species: *A. flagelliformis,* the well-known rat's tail cactus, is a typical plant for a farmhouse room. In each village, especially in southwest Germany, in the Alsace and in Switzerland, one sees it in the windows of the farmhouses and in the summer outside among oleander, lemon trees, angel's trumpet, and other tub plants, which love the warmth and the sun. *A. flagelliformis* forms many roundish, branched thin shoots with a diameter up to ⅝ inch (2 cm). The shoots can grow up to 39 inches (1 m) long. The ribs are only slightly developed. The areoles stand densely together and have 8 to 12 red-brown edge spines and 3 to 4 middle spines with yellow tips. The red to red-violet blossoms, which are especially large on the hybrid × *Helioporus smithii,* appear in large numbers in the early summer and are up to 3 inches (8 cm) long.

A. conzattii grows as a hanging plant or creeper and forms a few air roots. The shoots are about ¾-inch (2 cm) thick, equipped with 8 to 10 low, tubercled ribs, and are covered with 15 to 20 thin, light brown spines. The brick-red blossoms grow 3½ inches (9 cm) long.

A. flagriformis has shoots with 11 ribs and red middle spines on new branches, as well as dark violet blossoms up to 4 inches (10 cm) long.

A. martianus is equipped with ¾-inch-thick (18 mm) shoots. The approximately 8 ribs carry areoles with 6 to 8 bristly spines. The deep pink blossoms grow to be 4 inches (10 cm) long. It is recommended to tie this species, which grows strongly, onto a trellis.

For a long time, Aporocactus flagelliformis was one of the most widespread cacti, which is not surprising in view of the magnificent blossoms, which last up to four days. Today, for the most part only hybrids are in cultivation.

Ariocarpus fissuratus

Without blossoms, Ariocarpus fissuratus would hardly be distinguishable from its stony background, as the little plant on the right shows.

Astrophytum ornatum is decorated with white flakes and has typically high, edged ribs, with spine clusters, in contrast to the bishop's cap (A. myriostigma), which has no spines.

Ariocarpus fissuratus.

○ ☼ ▽ ʊ △

General notes: When they are not blooming, these cacti look as much as possible like their environment. They are gray-green, like the stones in their natural habitats, Texas and Mexico. Instead of ribs, they have spirally standing wart tubercles. The plants grow very slowly and may eventually reach 4 to 6 inches (10 to 15 cm) across.

Care: These cacti prefer warm locations with full sunlight. They are sensitive to humidity, should only be watered moderately, and should be kept completely dry during the winter. The soil has to be meager and very porous. New cacti are grown from seed. It is recommended that the seedlings be grafted onto *Pereskiopsis spathulata*.

Species: *A. fissuratus* has a flat, rosettelike body with fissured areoles and large, white to scarlet-red blossoms.

EXTRA TIP: Did you know that in the 19th century, the Russian prince Kotschoubey bought an *Ariocarpus* specimen for eight times its weight in gold? Since then, this "gold cactus" has been called *A. kotschoubeyanus*.

Ariocarpus species are also found under the name Roseocactus or Neogomesia.

Astrophytum

Astrophytum ornatum.

○ ○ 🌡 ▽ ʊ

General notes: *Astrophytum* come in many shapes and are quite beautiful. Unfortunately, they are almost extinct in their natural habitats of Texas and Mexico, where they grow up to 5 feet (150 cm) tall. In cultivation, they remain much smaller.

Care: Depending on the species, *Astrophytum* need either a sunny or half-shady spot that is always warm. The soil should be slightly acidic, humous, containing a little calcium sulfate, and mixed with clay and pumice. Water sparsely and keep dry during the winter at a temperature of 46 to 50°F (8 to 10°C). Transplant seedlings only if absolutely necessary, because they are very root sensitive. The ungrafted species blossom when they are as big as a fist; therefore, grafting is not necessary.

Species: *A. asterias* has a flat, globular, gray-green, symmetrical body without spines, with 7–8 wide ribs and large, white, feltlike areoles. The top is slightly woolly. The blossoms open up wide in the sun and are

Aztekium ritteri

Blossfeldia

about 1 inch (3 cm) long and up to 2 inches (5 cm) wide. They are lemon yellow on the inside. On the outside, they are shiny and the color of straw.

A. capricorne is commonly called the goat's horn cactus. The long, disorderly, tangled spines grow up to 4 inches (10 cm) long and completely envelop the globular plant body. The light to citrus yellow, shiny blossoms are especially big. They are colored scarlet red at the bottom.

A. myriostigma, the famous bishop's cap, has a globular to a longish body with a sunken top without spines. The body has 5 sharp-edged ribs (sometimes only 3–4, but frequently also 6–8). The surface is sprinkled with white hair flakes. The blossoms, up to 2½ inches (6 cm) wide, shine silkily.

A. myriostigma var. *nudum* has no flakes and the body is pure green. This species needs the half-shade, because without protection from the sun, it turns reddish.

A. ornatum is globular in its youth; it becomes column-shaped at an older age. The 8 ribs are prettily covered in arched stripes with little white flakes. They have long, straight yellowish to dark brown spines. The light yellow blossoms grow up to 3½ inches (9 cm) wide.

Aztekium ritteri.

General notes: The plant, of which only one species exists, originates in Mexico and it grows in groups. The individual plant body is flat, round, about 1 inch (3 cm) tall, and 2 inches (5 cm) in diameter. It grows extremely slowly. The main ribs are folded diagonally, very tightly. Narrow side ribs grow between the main ribs. The cactus has only a few short winding or crooked needles. The blossoms are dainty and light pink; the fruit are like berries and reddish. There is a variant with somewhat larger, long-stemmed blossoms.
Care: Difficult. In the summer, the plant needs to be warm and sunny, and it has to be watered a lot. In the winter, it has to be kept completely dry. As soil, use ground-up slate and sand with a lot of brick pieces and perlite to promote good drainage; avoid wet soil. Grafting is recommended for this slow-growing plant.

Blossfeldia liliputana.

General notes: These tiny cushion-shaped cacti come from Argentina and Bolivia. They grow between boulders on steep cliffs. Their color and shape is hardly distinguishable from a stone's. The individual plant has a diameter of ⅝-inch (1.6 cm) at the most and is flat. When they are extremely dry, they shrivel to millimeter-thick little disks, which swell up again in the rain. The mini-cacti have spirally arranged areoles. In the summer, the blossoms grow out of the plant's top.
Care: Difficult. *Blossfeldia* can only be kept under glass. As long as the plant bodies are swollen, hardly water at all. The soil should contain loam and should be acidic. Propagation by seed is difficult; but, when grafting is done, the plant degenerates.
Species: *B. liliputana*, *B. atroviridis*, and *B. minima* have white flowers when they are only ⅜-inch (10 mm) tall.

The stocky body of Aztekum ritteri crouches close to the surface. It has striking folded main ribs with side ribs standing in between.

Blossfeldia liliputana, the "tiny one," shows, in its miniature form, the complete beauty of a flowering cushion-shaped cactus. One clearly sees also the spiral arrangement of the little areole pads.

EXTRA TIP: *Blossfeldia* **can be rarely bought commercially.** *B. liliputana* **and** *B. minima* **are the easiest ones to get. Whoever is successful in growing another species can be proud to own a genuine rarity.**

Borzicactus

Browningia

Borzicactus morleyanus has slender, upright or bent sprouts and carmine-red blossoms up to 3 inches (7.5 cm) long with scarlet red filaments.

For Browningia hertlingiana, the synonym Azureocereus hertlingianus is more suitable, because of its appearance. The bright azure-blue bodies with their strong red needles are eye-catchers in any collection.

Borzicactus morleyanus.

General care: These magnificent column cacti from central and southern Ecuador can grow up to 5 feet (1.5 m) tall. They usually grow upright, but sometimes also are recumbent. The columns have diagonally grooved ribs, which are a bit thickened at the areoles. Colorful spines make the cacti interesting to look at. The pointy-petaled red day blossoms on a narrow calyx can grow up to 3¼ inches (8 cm) long. They appear in the summer.

Care: Relatively easy. *Borzicactus* have to be kept under glass, because the plants like warmth and sun. Water them frequently with calcium-free water. In the winter, keep dry at temperatures above 50°F (10°C).

Species: *B. humboldtii:* brown spines, carmine-red blossoms. *B. icosagonus:* yellow spines, orange blossoms. *B. roezlii:* bristly hair, dark carmine-red blossoms. *B. morleyanus:* whitish spines, red blossoms.

> **Borzicactus species also are found under *Seticereus* sometimes.**

Browningia hertlingiana.

General notes: *Browningia* species are treelike members of the subtribe Cereinae. In their native habitat, southern Peru and northern Chile, they grow up to 16 feet (5 m) tall. Their white blossoms open up at night. In cultivation, it is only practical to keep *Browningia* in their youth.

Care: The plants are rather robust and like to be in a sunny location or half-shade. The soil should be slightly acidic, with some loam mixed into the cactus soil. Water moderately in the summer. Provide proper drainage to avoid soil wetness. *Browningia* are sensitive to winter temperatures below 53°F (12°C).

Species: *B. hertlingiana,* with its bright blue shoots and tuberclelike thickenings at the areoles, is especially popular. In its youth, it has 3-inch-long (8 cm) yellow edge spines that have brown points.

> **Browningia hertlingiana is also known as *Azureocereus hertlingianus.***

Carnegia gigantea

Giant saguaro cactus

Carnegia gigantea.

Carnegia gigantea.

Carnegia gigantea, as it looks in its youth. The plant lover values it for its strong, dense spines.

Carnegia gigantea in its native habitat; this is how every Western fan knows it. The treelike giant cacti live for decades and flower only in old age.

General notes: These cacti grow up to 50 feet (15 m) tall. Their blossoms are the state flower of Arizona. We know them from many Western movies. The columnlike stems branch out into 6- to 10-foot-tall (2 to 3 m) candelabrum-shaped branches. The plants can form actual "forests." The few branches have a diameter of 12 to 26 inches (30 to 65 cm). The branches grow vertically and have 12 to 24 ribs. The brown areoles are densely covered with yellowish spines. The middle spines get to be up to 2¾ inches (7 cm) long. The typical "bat blossoms" are white. They sit at top of the crown and remain open day and night. The fruit grow to 3½ inches (9 cm) long and are edible when ripe. Large specimens of *Carnegia gigantea* store up to 790 gallons (3000 litres) of water and can survive for a long time without precipitation. The shallow roots develop a total length of up to 62 miles (100 km). In its natural habitat, *C. gigantea* is a useful plant. The woody body serves as building material; fruit and seeds are food products; and a beverage is made from its juicy pulp.

Care: Rather difficult. In cultivation, it grows very slowly—about 3 feet (1 m) in 30 years—and does not develop any flowers. The plant needs a light, sunny, and warm location, which is cool and sunny in winter. The soil should be porous, rich with nutrients, and slightly acidic. Propagate by seed.

EXTRA TIP:
The saguaro cactus is strictly protected. South of Phoenix, Arizona, a saguaro park has been created solely for this species.

Cephalocereus senilis
Old-man cactus

Cephalocereus senilis, the old-man cactus, with long, shaggy gray bristles, is cultivated because of its strange appearance. It only flowers in its natural habitat (central Mexico).

Cereus peruvianus var. monstrosus is a typical rock cactus. The bizarrely shaped plants reach a considerable size in cultivation and are suitable for planting by themselves.

Cephalocereus senilis.

General notes: In their native Mexico, *Cephalocereus* grow up to 50 feet (15 m) tall. In their youth, they look totally different than in their old age. The old-man cactus, as it is called, *Cephalocereus senilis*, appears in its youth as follows: a dense coat of long white bristle hair envelops the plant body. The areoles stand densely together on the 20 to 30 flat ribs. Out of them come 2 to 5 spines and up to 4¾-inch-long (12 cm) hairs, which entwine. In cultivation, the plants seldom bloom.
Care: Difficult, and only under glass. They need full light and high air humidity. In the winter, temperatures should be above 59°F (15°C). When it is cool, they are very sensitive to soil humidity. Propagate by seed.

> **The genus *Cephalocereus* is disputed. Certainly the genus *Haseltonia*, with *H. columnatrajani* (syn. *C. hoppenstedtii*), belongs in this category. Whether the same holds true for other columnar *Cereus*, such as *Pilocereus*, *Pilosocereus*, *Neobuxbaumia*, and others, has not been clarified.**

Cereus

Cereus peruvianus var. monstrosus

General notes: These mostly treelike or shrublike column cacti are rather attractive, but they don't grow as tall in other places as they do in their South American homeland. They grow quickly and easily, and for collectors, they soon become too big. They have widely branched crowns, and blossoms that open up at night from June to September. Some *Cereus* species are good bases for grafting.
Care: Easy. All *Cereus* species need a sunny, warm location during the summer. If they are kept totally dry during winter, they can even put up with a little frost. In Mediterranean countries, they are frequently planted outside, where they come through the winter without problems. The plants are rather modest. They need a slightly acidic, porous soil, containing loam and humus, and have to be generously fertilized and watered. Monstrous forms are susceptible to mealy bugs and scales. Propagate by seed or cuttings, which root easily.

Chamaecereus silvestrii

Peanut cactus

Species: *C. jamacaru* in its native Brazil grows up to 33 feet (10 m) tall. It has a short trunk and a branched crown. The new shoots are light green to blue-green. Crown and areoles are yellow-brown; the spines are yellowish to brownish and strong. The blossoms are pure white and up to 10 inches (25 cm) long. They open up at night. Recently, there are also dwarf forms of the monstrous rock cactus, *C. jamacaru* var. *monstrosus*.

C. peruvianus and its growth anomaly, var. *monstrosus*, also a rock cactus, has denser spines than *C. jamacaru*. The spines are brown-red. The ribs are flat; in the monstrous form, they are often strongly broken through. This cactus does not tolerate any calcium.

C. forbesii is an attractive species with a gray-green shoots, white felty areoles, and horn-colored spines.

All the above-mentioned species, as well as the rock cactus, are plants for beginners; they are robust and easy to take care of, and they are frequently used as bases for grafting.

Chamaecereus silvestrii.

Chamaecereus 'Fire Chief.'

Chamaecereus silvestrii, with its bright-red blossoms, has one disadvantage: the abundant sprouts break off very easily. Cures have been sought through cultivation and crossing.

Chamaecereus 'Fire Chief' is such a cultivar, a real blooming wonder! The compact, shorter shoots, pushed together in dense groups, are almost completely covered with dozens of flowers.

General notes: This popular, undemanding, and strongly hybridized cactus species is a native of South America. Anyone who has seen it in full bloom in its native habitat in the Andes of Argentina between Salta and Tucumán necessarily wants to cultivate it. Soft, fleshy, finger-shaped, light-green shoots grow in small, dense groups. The shoots break off easily, but quickly grow roots again. In direct sunlight, they turn red. The shoots have 6 to 9 ribs with densely sanding areoles and very short, soft white prickles. The bright red blossoms are 1½ inches (4 cm) long and open widely during the day.

Care: Easy. In order to produce a voluptuous flower in April or May, the plant needs a dry winter period somewhat above 32°F (0°C) in an unheated hotbed or greenhouse. If they have been hardened, hybrids of this cactus species can, under certain circumstances, be kept outside during the winter. There are cactus lovers who keep them planted in the ground outside in a stone garden. The soil should be slightly acidic and humous, and should be mixed with brick chips and perlite. In the summer, these cacti need to be fertilized a lot and watered regularly. The dwarf column cactus is susceptible to red spider mites if the air is too dry or warm. Propagation using the easily breakable shoots is not a problem.

Species: There are numerous crossings of *Chamaecereus silvestrii* with *Lobivia*, above all with *Lobivia famatimensis*. These hybrids have firmer, strong limbs, which do not break off so easily. They produce a whole palette of attractive blossom colors, from yellow to orange and all red shades to violet.

EXTRA TIP: The most beautiful spines develop on the dwarf column cactus when it is planted in a warm season in a light place directly outside.

Cleistocactus

Cleistocactus smaragdiflorus.

Cleistocactus in the succulent house of the Palm Garden in Frankfurt, Germany.

General notes: All species are extremely popular, because they are diverse, because their spines are very colorful and attractive, and because they flower strikingly and abundantly. The native habitat of this genus is South America, from Argentina to Peru.

Cleistocactus form not very tall shrubs with thin, multiply-ribbed branches. The areoles are separated by cross ribs. The spines of most species are as fine as hair. Some species have stronger, longer spines and flower abundantly from the early spring until summer in white, yellow, red, orange, carmine-red, and even in green. The slightly hairy blossoms stick out of the plant in rows, like fingers.

Care: Easy. All *Cleistocactus* are fairly undemanding. They like to stay in a sunny location with moist soil and a relatively high air humidity. They prefer to be planted directly outside or to be in a summery room with fresh air from June until mid-September. During the growth period, they need to be sprayed or misted regu-larly in the evening. In the winter, keep them at 50°F (10°C) and never let them dry out completely. The soil should be very nutritious and porous. Propagation by seed is not a problem, and cuttings easily grow roots.

Species: Over 20 species of the genus are known. The most beautiful ones are as follows: *C. baumannii*, with dark green shoots up to 6½ feet (2 m) tall, 14 to 16 ribs, and long spines with light points. The S-shaped blossoms are bright red.

C. smaragdiflorus, with small, partially recumbent, thick branches, which bloom after reaching 10 inches (25 cm) in length. The blossoms are red with an emerald-green border. The fruit are attractive and light red.

C. straussii is one of the most beautiful species. It grows upright, branches out, and blooms from a height of about 3 feet (1 m). The slender, columnlike shoots carry long, hair-fine, white bristle needles with light yellow middle spines. The blossoms are up to 3½ inches (9 cm) long and are ruby-colored.

Copiapoa

Copiapoa cinerea.

🌡 ⊟ 🗲 🜍 🌱

General notes: The barrel cacti of this genus live on the coastal deserts of north and central Chile. They grow near the coast on rocky or stony terraces and are exposed to extreme sunlight and to winds that dry them out. In order to survive the extreme climate there, they have developed coverings of thick, whitish wax layers, which give them their typical floury or chalk-white appearance. Globular species belong to the genus *Copiapoa*, which also form cushions and such, and grow in old age into the shape of columns. They branch at the base in clumps and only bloom as large specimens. The plant bodies are green, gray, brownish, and floury white. The spines are white, brown, or black. The large yellow day blossoms have a pleasant scent in some species.

Care: Relatively difficult. The location has to be very warm and bright, and it has to be in direct sun. The best way to keep them is under glass. In the spring and late summer, their water require-ment is very great. Between these times are dry rest periods. In the winter, on the other hand, keep the plants absolutely dry and at temperatures above 46°F (8°C). *Copiapoa* grow in mineral, porous soil that should be mixed with gravel. The roots need a lot of room, so make sure that the pots are large enough! Propagation is from seed. Plants grown from seed are, by the way, much easier to care for than the ones that are bought. Through grafting, cultivation is even more secure.

Species: *C. cinerea* is globular, later becoming short-columned, with a chalk-white body. It has mostly black spines and yellow blossoms.

C. grandiflora has brownish black to gray spines. The blossoms are light yellow inside, red outside.

C. haseltoniana has a body without a chalk-white covering, but has a brown, woolly crown.

C. humilis is very little, with ¾ inch-long (2 cm) yellow blossoms.

C. krainziana is the most beautiful species. The body is gray-green, and the long bristly spines are whitish.

C. lembecki has a whitish blue-green body. The areoles are gray-black.

C. montana has a wide, round, blue-green body with sturdy shoots up to 8 inches (20 cm) tall. The plants have 10 to 17 ribs, which are thickened around the brownish white areoles like tubercles. The spines are brown-red to black. The blossoms are 1½ inches (4 cm) long, cream yellow, and have a pleasant odor.

Corryocactus

with Erdisia

Corryocactus.

◻ ◐ 🌡 ⊟

General notes: This species is one with the longest spines—up to 8 inches (20 cm) long. The plants branch at the base; the strong shoots grow, depending on the species, upright or creeping. The ribs are strongly swollen or tubercle-shaped around the areoles. Most of the species grow up to 6½ feet tall (2 m) in their South American habitat. *Erdisia* plants grow up to 10 feet tall (3 m). The large blossoms may be yellow, orange, or scarlet.

Care: Easy. *Corryocactus* need a warm location under glass and sandy, very nutritious, and slightly acidic soil. In the summer, sprinkle or mist them a lot and water regularly. Provide proper drainage—wet soil because of blocked drainage is deadly! *Corryocactus* and *Erdisia* are, when grafted, good cacti for beginners.

Species: *C. aureispina* (light red); *C. ayopayanus* (orange); *C. charazanensis* (salmon pink); *C. krausii* (yellow); *C. melanotrichus* (crimson); *C. perezianus* (pink); *C. pulquinensis* (red-orange).

Copiapoa cinerea is translated as "ash-gray Copiapoa," whereby the body color is well-described. In old age, the plant becomes column-shaped.

Although this is a relatively young and small specimen of Corryocactus, one can get a definite premonition of danger from the long needles of this genus.

EXTRA TIP: *Corryocactus* is pretty in its natural habitat; in cultivation, even under glass, there is only a small reflection of its real beauty.

Coryphantha

Denmoza

Discocactus

Coryphantha vivipara.

Denmoza erythrocephala.

Discocactus horstii.

The relatively large flowers of Cory-phantha vivipara are created centrally, as with all species of the genus. Unfortunately, the groove of the warts, which is just as typical, is not recog-nizable in this photo.

Denmoza erythrocephala, "the red-headed Denmoza," owes its name to the fox-red spines, which do not stand out too well between the hairs.

Discocactus horstii shows the typical habitus of this flat, globular genus. The plant only grows to be ¾-inch (2 cm) tall. The cephalium, which stays just as flat, is covered by the flowers that come out of it.

General notes: This genus, which is rich in species, has very large blossoms in comparison to its body size. It has species specifically suitable for the advanced collector, but there are also ones for the beginner.

Care: The species that inhabit the desert are sensitive. Use a soil that contains a lot of nutrient salt and calcium sulfate, but no humus. In the summer, water very little. The thick-fleshed grassland species accept a less porous soil that is slightly acidic. They need more watering, a lot of sun, and fresh air in the summer. During the winter, keep them dry, light, and cool. It is possible to grow these cacti from seed, but frequently they have to be grafted later on.

Species: *C. vivipara* and *C. columnaris*, blossoms dark purple. *C. cornifera* (syn. *C. radians*), lemon yellow. *C. andreae*, *C. clava*, and *C. compacta*, yellow. *C. elephantidens* and *C. ramillosa*, pink. *C. obscura*, orange. *C. ottonis*, white.

General notes: The species *D. erythrocephala* from northwestern Argentina is well known among cactus lovers. At first it grows globularly, but with increasing age, it becomes column-shaped. The plant body is densely covered with fox-red spines that are later mixed with white bristle hairs. The red blossoms are 2¾ inches (7 cm) long. They have extremely short crown leaves and hardly open up.

Care: Relatively simple. In the summer, the plants want to be where it is very warm and sunny, and they want to be watered a lot. During the winter, keep them cold and almost dry. The soil should be porous and purely mineral. Propagation is by seed.

Species: Besides *D. erythrocephala* and *D. rhodantha*, a hybrid × *Cleistocactus strausii* is very appealing.

General notes: Collectors consider these barrel cacti of this genus from South America to be rarities. The plant bodies are wide and round. They flower out of real crown cephalium, and then end their vegetative growth. The large blossoms are whitish, funnel-shaped, and have a strong smell. The blossoms open up at night.

Care: Difficult. The location has to be airy and warm. During the winter it should be absolutely dry, light, and kept at 54° to 59°F (12° to 15°C). The soil should be porous, mineral, and mixed with a little bit of quartz sand. Water only with calcium-free, slightly acidic water. Wet soil because of improper drainage is deadly for these species, and grafting is recommended.

Species: *D. horstii*; gray-green with very small, clawlike needles and a pure white blossom.

D. hartmannii; dark green body, white blossoms, and smells like lily of the valley.

Dolichothele

Dolichothele longimamma.

General notes: Representatives of the genus *Dolichothele* are found from Texas to Mexico. They all have unusually long, soft warts and relatively soft spines. There are large- and small-blossomed species, all of which bloom reliably, long, and wonderfully.
Care: Easy. Even beginners are successful with this genus. The plants desire a location in the half-shade that is warm and moderately humid. Keep dry and cool but not under 41°F (5°C) during the winter rest period. The soil should be humous, slightly acidic, nutritious, porous, and should contain loam. Water sparsely. Propagation through division is simplest. It is also possible to grow them from seed.
Species: *D. baumii:* up to ½-inch (1 cm) long warts; fine spines, and large yellow strong-smelling blossoms.

D. camptotricha has small flowers; the crown leaves grow white.

D. longimamma has individual or multisprouted bodies with warts that are 1 to 2¾ inches (3 to 7 cm) long and yellow blossoms of up to 2½ inches (6 cm).

D. surculosa proliferates abundantly and forms a lawn. The blossoms are small, funnel-shaped, and interestingly colored. The sepals are chrome yellow with pink stripes on the back; the crown leaves are sulfur yellow with red points and orange-colored back stripes.

> This genus is sometimes also classified with *Mammillaria*.

Echinocactus

Barrel cactus

Echinocactus ingens.

The pretty, pleasant-smelling blossoms of Dolichothele longimamma hide the extraordinary shape of this plant with its long, nipple-shaped, soft warts and long spines.

Echinocactus ingens is not as well known as its brother, the famous golden barrel cactus (Echinocactus grusonii), but nevertheless it resembles it quite a bit.

General notes: These globular or short, cylindrical cacti range from the southern states of the USA to Mexico. They become very large and have coarse, densely-standing spines and yellow blossoms (only *E. horizonthalonius* has pink-colored blossoms) when it grows older. They rarely bloom in cultivation.
Care: *E. horizonthalonius*, *E. polycephalus*, and others are difficult. Some are easy, for example *E. grusonii*. Locate fully in the sun where it is very warm and airy. In the summer they should be outside. Water and fertilize regularly. Keep dry during the winter rest period, and not below 50°F (10°C). The soil needs to be very porous, sandy, and loamy–humous. Propagate by seed.
Species: *E. grusonii*, the golden barrel cactus, with golden-yellow, dense thorns, is widespread. *E. ingens*, *E. platyacanthus* var. *grandis*, and *Homalocephala texensis*, also classified in this genus, are not recommended for beginners.

> **EXTRA TIP:** *Echinocactus grusonii* was almost made extinct in its natural habitat and was therefore placed under protection. The attractive cactus with the whitish yellow thorns and the bright yellow woolly crown can also grow into a giant globe in cultivation if it is planted in the ground bed of a sunny greenhouse.

Echinocereus

Hedgehog cactus
Pitaya

The salmon-colored, long-tubed blossoms of Echinocereus salm-dyckianus grow laterally on the shoots that are often recumbent, with 7 to 9 slightly bayed ribs.

Echinocereus subinermis, the "almost unarmed one," has yellow blossoms. The species is called "unarmed" because the spines are rather sparse and very small.

In Echinocereus pentalophus, the large, wide flowers with the light throats contrast nicely with the fresh green of the shoots and the short needles.

In Echinocereus pectinatus var. rigidissimus, the comblike, close-lying needles are especially strong, and they vary in their color by zones. The sepals of the blossoms are very small.

Edible red fruit develops out of the scarlet-red blossoms of Echinocereus triglochidiatus.

General notes: This genus from the southwest USA and Mexico, with over 60 species, is highly valued by cactus lovers for the intense colors of the magnificent day blossoms. There are small, globular *Echinocereus*; short, columned ones; those that form a ground cover; and sparsely branched species. The spines also are very diverse.

Care: Easy. In the summer, an airy location in bright sun; well watered when it is hot. In the winter: light, cool, and absolutely dry conditions. These cacti grow best when planted freely outside in very nutritious, well-drained soil. Some will survive the winter outside. All are sensitive to red spider mites. Propagate by seed or sprouts.

Species: *E. dasyacanthus* has yellow blossoms. *E. pectinatus* and its variation, var. *rigidissimus*, have spine zones that vary in color and very large reddish blossoms. *E. pentalophus* creates a ground cover, flowers abundantly, and has carmine-red blossoms. *E. salm-dyckianus*, forms groups and has carrot-colored blossoms. *E. scheerii* has rose-red blossoms. *E. stramineus* produces huge red blossoms. *E. subinermis* has yellow blossoms. *E. triglochidiatus* is winter-hardy under certain conditions. It is strongly branched, it produces scarlet blossoms, and its fruit is edible. *E. fitschii* is especially willing to flower.

Echinocereus salm-dyckianus.

Echinocereus subinermis.

Echinocereus pentalophus.

E. pectinatus var. rigidissimus.

Echinocereus triglochidiatus.

Echinocereus stramineus.

Echinocereus stramineus creates colonies up to 6½ feet (2 m) in diameter. The purple-colored blossoms are up to 4¾ inches (12 cm) in size.

Echinocereus dasyacanthus, the "coarsely prickly one," usually grows individually in short, cylindrical, thick columns up to 12 inches (30 cm) tall. The light-yellow striped blossoms only open up in the afternoon.

Echinocereus dasyacanthus.

EXTRA TIP: *Echinocereus* are ideal beginner cacti for colorful, merry plantings.

Echinofossulocactus   Echinomastus

The lamellar cacti, to which Echinofossulo-cactus pentacanthus belongs, are meadow inhabitants of the Central American mountains.

Like all Echinomastus species, Echinomastus macdowellii has a strikingly beautiful spine coat and is, in addition, the only species that grows ungrafted.

Echinofossulocactus pentacanthus.

General notes: The common characteristics of this genus of Mexican barrel cacti are small growth, thin, wavy ribs and paperlike, flattened, long middle spines. The blossoms appear in the spring.
Care: Easy. In the summer, the plants require sun or half-shade; cultivation is also possible outside. During the winter, keep them almost dry at 46° to 54°F (8 to 12°C). The soil needs to be porous, humous, nutritious, and slightly acidic. Propagate by seed. Grafting results in the loss of the typical spines.
Species: *E. arrigens*, globular, stretched body, up to 60 small ribs and purple-violet blossoms. *E. lamellosus*, blue-green body and over 30 lamellar ribs; middle spine, up to 1 inch (3 cm) long; red blossoms, violet inside. *E. pentacanthus*, spines usually bent upwards; violet blossoms with a white edge. *E. violaciflorus*, globular, elongated body, 35 ribs, a carinated middle thorn, ringlets, and an attractive white blossom with a violet middle.

> **EXTRA TIP:** *Echinofossulo-cactus* species are variable and undemanding, therefore well suited for beginners.

Echinomastus macdowellii.

General notes: The short cylindrical or globular cacti from the deserts of northern Mexico and the southwestern United States have ribs that are highly divided into tubercles. Behind the spine bundle are the long areoles. These are felty in plants that are capable of blooming. The blossoms, near the crown, are relatively small, bell-shaped, and, in most species, are white to pink.
Care: Difficult. The cacti love the warmth and can only be grown directly under glass, perhaps with a little bit of shade. Keep absolutely dry in the winter. The slightly acidic soil should be mineral to sandy with a slight amount of calcium sulfate. The plants are very sensitive to cool humidity; therefore, water very carefully in the summer. Grafted specimens are not as sensitive; only they are recommended for beginners.
Species: *E. erectocentrus* grows short and cylindrical. The blossoms are madder red.

E. intertextus has edge spines that lie close to the body and are entwined. Most of the time these plants have erect middle spines. They are all light to reddish and have purple-colored blossoms with white edges.

E. johnsonii develops red spines and flesh-colored blossoms.

E. macdowellii is wide and globular. It is yellow and felty at the crown and grows red funnel-shaped blossoms.

E. unguispinus grows greenish flowers.

Echinopsis

Sea-urchin cactus

⚪ ◦ 🌡 🪣 🌿

General notes: These indestructible cacti from South America have sat on windowsills in cities and in the country for over 100 years. Without needing much care, they bloom and grow seeds, which produce bastards almost exclusively. Pure wild forms have become very rare. Through a targeted hybrid cultivation, the color of the blossoms has been enhanced. They come out in the spring and summer and open up at night. The blossoms are long-tubed, up to 10 inches (25 cm) long. They are mostly white, more rarely pink. The plant bodies are globular to longish; later on, they are short-columned. The plants grow as individuals or as multiple shoots.

Care: Easy. The location should be warm. In the summer, it should be sunny with some slight protection from the full sunshine, preferably outside where the spines grow especially beautifully. Under glass, they have to be kept humid. For the winter rest period, keep them very cool and dry. Only then will they bloom. If necessary, keep them in the basement. For strong growth and many blossoms, the plants need a porous, nutritious soil, which has to be fertilized frequently.

Species: *E. eyriesii* has a globular body. It grows first as an individual, then with many shoots and long white blossoms. From this and the following species, hybrids originate.

Echinopsis hybrid.

Echinopsis multiplex.

Echinopsis 'Paramount.'

E. *bridgesii*, E. *rhodotricha*, and E. *tubiflora* also have white blossoms. E. *multiplex* grows up to 12 inches (30 cm) tall. It has narrow edges on top with large, white areoles and long, light-brown needles. The blossom is white to pink, which holds true also for E. *oxygona* and E. *werdermannii*.

Day-blooming *Pseudolobivia* are frequently classified with *Echinopsis* and also have very beautiful hybrids.

E. *aurea* grows to be about 4 inches (10 cm) tall with yellow blossoms about 3½ inches (9 cm) long.

E. *kermesina* is up to 7 inches (18 cm) long with carmine-red blossoms.

Other species: E. *kratochviliana*, pure white; E. *calorubra*, orange-red; E. *frankii*, light red-violet.

Eight magnificent light-pink blossoms on a plant as big as a tennis ball are no rarity among Echinopsis hybrids.

Echinopsis multiplex is one of the most indestructible species. Our grandmothers had them on their windowsills. The pure-white blossom hints at the fact that this is a bastard, because the blossom color of the original form is pinkish red.

This is one of the magnificently blooming 'Paramount' hybrids of Echinopsis. The blossoms are more strongly colored than the rather pale white to red-tinted ones of the wild plants.

Epiphyllum Hybrids

Orchid cactus

Various magnificent Epiphyllum hybrids. Top, 'Starflight.' Middle, left, 'Roter Stern.' Middle, right, 'Andromeda.' Bottom left, 'Jennifer Ann.' Bottom right, 'Desert Rose.'

General notes: These beautiful cacti grow as epiphytes in their warm, humid tropical habitats from Mexico to South America; therefore, in cultivation, they are grown as hanging plants. The green shoots, which have three to four sides and are round at the base, only have spines as seedlings. The end branches are mostly flat, hanging, and dentated at the edges. Old plant parts become woody. The splendid, diversified blossoms of the hybrids open up at night and stay open for about two days. The blossoms of the wild forms are white to reddish. They appear, depending on the species and variety, in the early spring up to the late summer. Later on, they change into striking red fruit.

Care: Relatively easy. They need shade or half-shade, but they must still have light. In the summer, the plants like it best outside. A lot of light during the winter prevents thin, narrow, winter shoots or "spears" from being created, which would have to be cut off. In the winter, keep at 50 to 59°F (10 to 15°C) in constantly slightly moist soil. The temperature may also be 41°F (5°C), but then the soil must be kept dry. During the time of growth, water them regularly. If they get too dry, the blossom buds fall off. The best soil is sandy humous soil with a lot of peat. If the soil is too heavy or dries out too often, the sensitive roots rot. This

'Starflight.'

'Roter Stern.'

'Andromeda.'

'Jennifer Ann.'

'Desert Rose.'

'Kitty Hawk.'

'Day Dream.'

'Honeycomb.'

'Monastery Garden.'

'Pegasus.'

is especially true of the tropical species. *Epiphyllum* are particularly vulnerable to nematodes and viruses. Symptoms include root cysts or, in the case of viruses, white-green spots, brown coloration, and bending of the youngest shoots. Infected plants cannot be saved. *Epiphyllum* are grown from cuttings.

Species: Synonyms also cover *Rhipsalidopsis* species. More important than the rarely cultivated botanical species *E. phyllanthum*, *E. crenatum*, or *E. anguligerum* (fishbone cactus), which all bloom whitish to reddish, are the hybrids, which bloom magnificently in all variations. Some of the hybrids are closely related to *Nopalxochia*.

Hybrids: Further attractive *Epiphyllum* variations are: 'Acapulco Sunset' (orange); 'Adam' (cream white), 'Agatha' (pink); 'Albert Pike' (white); 'Albertine' (light violet); 'Bohemienne' (bright red); 'Bolero' (red with violet); 'Carnival' (orange with violet); 'Clown' (white, pink, and red); 'First Prom' (light violet); 'Forty Niner' (cream yellow with golden yellow); 'Frances C.' (lemon yellow); 'King Midas' (yellow with brown-orange); 'Mexa Kelly' (snow-white).

More beauties from the remarkable assortment of the Epiphyllum. Top, 'Kitty Hawk.' Middle left, 'Day Dream.' Middle right, 'Honeycomb.' Bottom left, 'Monastery Gardens.' Bottom right, 'Pegasus.'

The term "leaf cactus" (Phyllocactus), which botanically refers only to the day-blooming hybrids of *Nopalxochia*, *Heliocereus*, *Selenicereus*, and others, became a common term also for the shrublike *Epiphyllum* species, because of their long, edgy, leaflike shoots.

Epithelantha

Eriosyce

Escobaria

Epithelantha micromeris.

Eriosyce ceratistes.

Escobaria tuberculosa.

General notes: These slow-growing, small, group-forming cacti come from western and northern Texas. With their small tubercles, the round to globular plants resemble the *Mammillaria*. Their blossoms are not created in a wreath out of the axils, but out of the youngest areoles in the more-or-less woolly crown. The spines lie close to the body, or protrude slightly.
Care: Difficult. Can be kept successfully only at a location in full sunlight and under glass. Water little and only in warm weather. During the winter rest period, the plant should be kept absolutely dry. The soil must be slightly acidic to neutral and contain calcium sulfate. The plants grow best when grafted, but they easily degenerate.
Species: *E. micromeris*, with its tiny, spirally arranged tubercles and white spines that lie close to the body, is best known. It creates pale pink blossoms out of a tuft of hair in the middle of the crown. *E. polycephala* branches into several heads.

General notes: These very large barrel cacti from the Cordillera in Chile are rarely seen in collections. Because there is such a wealth of shapes, it is not quite clear if we are dealing with several species or with varieties of one species. The plant bodies grow up to 3 feet (1 m) tall and up to 20 inches (50 cm) wide. The spines are black, yellow, or gray. In the crown, a woolly tuft of hair is created, which is interspersed with spines. The blossom colors range from pink to medium red.
Care: Relatively easy. Location in the summer should be very light and warm with a lot of watering. During the winter rest period keep them light, cool, and dry. The soil has to be light, but nutritious. Repeat fertilizing can't do any harm.
Species: *E. ceratistes*, with coarse, clawlike upward-bent spines and red blossoms with short tubes. Another species is *E. bruchii*.

General notes: These dainty cacti, which resemble *Mammillaria*, come from western Texas and New Mexico. In their youth, they are tiny. When they grow older, they become globular or cylindrical and form groups. The spines are thin and needlelike; the little blossoms in the crown have different colors.
Care: Difficult. In order for the plants to bloom, a lot of sun and heat are needed. Water only a little, but regularly; in midsummer, with a pause. During the winter rest period, provide complete dryness and temperatures from 43° to 50°F (6 to 10C°). Use a porous soil with a lot of nutrient salts, some peat, and calcium sulfate. Propagation is by seed or sprout grafting.
Species: *E. roseana* and *E. runyonii* have purple blooms; *E. lloydii*, greenish; *E. emskoetteriana*, white; *E. rigida*, violet; *E. zilziana*, yellow.
   E. chaffeyi has pink to cream-colored blossoms; *E. hesteri* has light purple ones; and *E. tuberculosa*, pink ones.

Espostoa

Espostoa lanata.

General notes: These species, which are already very attractive as seedlings, originate in Ecuador and Peru. Whether they are shrublike or tree-shaped, all have a more or less dense, white, woolly coat of hair. The spines are whitish, yellow, or reddish. When they are old enough to bloom, a tight woolly, white, yellow, or brown cephalium is created laterally at the shoot; white blossoms grow out of it.
Care: Easy. The plants need full sun and warmth in a greenhouse. Sprinkle or mist them frequently. Water only a little and only in warm weather; overwintering dry and cool. The soil should be loose and nutritious. Propagate by seed.
Species: *E. lanata* ('Cotton Ball') has shoots that are surrounded by white hair.
E. melanostele (syn. *Pseudoespostoa melanostele*) has dense white woolly hair.
E. nana (syn. *P. nana*) is completely enveloped in a silky white hair coat.

> Some *Espostoa* species are also listed under *Pseudoespostoa*.

Eulychnia

Eulychnia ritteri.

General notes: Because of their magnificent spines, the shrublike or tree-shaped *Eulychnia* from Chile belong to the most beautiful column cacti. Young plants stand out because of the strong white or grey areolar felt with its long hair. The spines are often long and coarse. The white blossoms very rarely grow in cultivation.
Care: Easy. Locate in bright sun in the summer, but keep them moderately humid, especially in the early fall, which is their main growth period. Provide proper drainage to avoid wet soil. Sprinkle in the evening with cold (!) water. Use a nutritious, porous soil. Fast growth is only achieved through grafting.
Species: *E. iquiquensis* is the most widespread one.
E. ritteri has very densely standing areoles with shaggy felt; thin, brownish edge spines; and long middle spines.
E. spinibarbis has areoles that are far apart with a lot of white hair in its youth.

Ferocactus

Ferocactus acanthodes.

General notes: This genus from the southern USA and Mexico has an unusual number of growth forms. Besides columns without branches, there are barrel-sized globes, flat disks, and huge cushions. Many have striking, strong spines, which can be hooklike, bent, twisted, or like ringlets. The yellow to orange blossoms only appear in large plants. Some species produce edible fruit.
Care: Difficult. Locate outside in full sun or under glass without full sun. Water regularly, but sparsely. Provide proper drainage to avoid wet soil. Use a sandy, loamy, porous soil. During the winter rest period, give it light and keep it absolutely dry at 50 to 57°F (10 to 14°C). Propagate with seed.
Species: *F. acanthodes*, up to 4¾ inches (12 cm) long, with pink or yellowish middle spines. *F. glaucescens*, with gold-yellow spines. *F. histrix*, with amber spines. *F. latispinus* has relatively small, ringed edge spines and red, flattened middle spines.

Among the many lovely Espostoa, Espostoa lanata may be the most beautiful. When they are young, their bodies are braided with white wool and look like cotton balls.

On a Eulychnia ritteri, the felty areoles look like rows of cotton wadding. The middle spines, which jut out from the areoles, grow up to 2½ inches (6 cm) long.

The long whitish, pink, light red, or yellowish spines of Ferocactus acanthodes suit the plant so well that blossoms aren't even missed.

> **EXTRA TIP:** *Espostoa* are jewels in any collection. Although blossoms are rarely achieved in cultivation, this genus is fascinating because of its dense hair web. Seedlings, by the way, grow well ungrafted, although very slowly. It is faster to graft them onto *Pereskiopsis*.

Frailea

Gymnocactus

Frailea castanea.

Gymnocactus beguinii.

General notes: This genus of dwarf globe cacti from the middle of South America includes species that are cleistogamous (see p. 26). The yellow blossoms open up only when the weather is extraordinarily hot and sunny. The bodies of these pretty, small cacti are light green to brown with flat ribs and tubercle rows that do not stand out very much. They sprout usually when they get old, but even then they need very little room.

Care: Relatively easy. Locate in the summer in a warm, not too dry place in half-shade. They can take mist very well. Keep cool in the winter. Shrinkage because of dryness does not do any harm. *Frailea* need a coarse, sandy, mineral, somewhat humous, nutritious soil. Propagate by seed. Grafting is unnecessary.

Species: *F. pulcherrima*, with light needles.

F. castanea, with a red-brown body and strikingly large yellow blossoms.

F. grahliana makes many shoots; brownish green.

General notes: These pretty globe cacti have fine and mostly light-colored spines and wool in the crown. They grow up to 6 inches (15 cm) tall. Only a few species sprout; some have storage roots. The ribs are clearly visible. The blossoms are only medium-sized, and they are predominantly purple, pink, or white.

Care: Difficult; not suitable for beginners. Locate in a hot, sunny, airy place. Water carefully in the summer. Improper drainage is damaging. Keep absolutely dry in the winter rest period at 43° to 50°F (6° to 10°C). Use very porous soil, containing 50% pumice stone and perlite. If grown indoors, graft onto *Trichocereus spachianus*.

Propagate by seed.

Species: *G. beguinii*, with a blue-green body, white woolly areoles, and violet blossoms.

G. gielsdorfianus, with a flat yellow to blue-gray body, spirally placed tubercles, and white blossoms.

G. horripilus forms groups and has purple-colored blossoms.

G. knuthianus, a sprouting species with a shiny, dark-green body, white spines, and light lilac-pink blossoms.

G. mandragora, with thick storage roots and white pink-striped blossoms.

G. valdezianus is very little. Its hairy, pinnate spines lie close to the body. The blossoms are violet-pink.

Gymnocalycium

Gymnocalycium mihanovichii var. friedrichii f. rubra

Gymnocalycium baldianum.

Gymnocalycium gibbosum.

○ ○ 🌡 🗑

General notes: *Gymnocalycium* are native to South America. They are ideal collector's items, with which even beginners can enjoy success. There are over 100 species of these robust globe cacti. They bloom from spring to fall in very beautiful colors. Their globular bodies usually grow individually and sprout very rarely.

They are small, but some are up to 12 inches (30 cm) tall, flattened, and equipped with distinct ribs, most of which have tubercles. The blossoms, which are close to the crown and have scales, are large, bell-shaped, and remain open for several days.

Care: Easy. The location should be airy, but protected from the full sunshine. During the winter rest period keep them not entirely dry at 46° to 54°F (8° to 12°C). The soil should be humous: 2 parts humus and 1 part loamy sand. Water moderately in the summer and keep fertilizing. Propagation by seed is without problems. Keep grafted cacti humid, warm and shaded in humous soil for 10–14 days. Water evenly.

Species: *G. andreae* has a dark blue-green body with a touch of bronze, few spines, sulfur-yellow blossoms.

G. baldianum has a small blue-green body with a storage root and purple blossoms.

G. bruchii is only 1¼ inches (3.5 cm) tall and sprouts well. It makes dainty bell blossoms in all shades of pink.

G. capillaense have wide, globular, sprouting bodies with light spines and white to pale pink blossoms.

G. damsii has a flat, light to dark green globe-shaped body and white blossoms.

G. gibbosum is 24 inches tall (60 cm) with long, bent spines and white blossoms.

G. mihanovichii has a gray-green to red-brown body, with banded ribs, long spines, and greenish blossoms. The blossoms of variety var. *friedrichii* are pink. There are chloroplast-free red, pink, yellow, violet, and multicolored mutants of *friedrichii*. They are grafted onto *Hylocereus trigonus*.

G. quehlianum is gray-green with a touch of red. The flat globular body has storage roots and makes pure white blossoms with red centers.

Grafted mutations such as the one at left are made from *Gymnocalycium mihanovichii var. friedrichii f. rubra*. The red or other-colored scions make offsets easily.

Gymnocalycium baldianum stands out because of its purpled-red blossom. It has a water-storing root.

The ribs of *Gymnocalycium gibbosum* are ½- to ¾-inch high (1.5 cm) and have sharp cross grooves. The typically scaly, white blossoms are up to 2½ inches (6.5 cm) tall.

Haageocereus

Hamatocactus

Haageocereus versicolor is a column cactus that should be part of every collection. The coloration of the needles changes in zones, from yellow at the bottom to fox-red at the crown.

Hamatocactus hamatacanthus has spines that are red or speckled at first. They are long and partially hooklike. The plant has very attractive large yellow blossoms with red centers. In contrast to Hamatocactus setispinus, the globular fruit is green, not red.

Haageocereus versicolor.

General notes: These colorfully and densely spined column cacti are from the west side of the Peruvian Andes. They grow up to 10 feet (3 m) tall. Depending on the species, the columns grow upright or recumbent. They have fine or coarse yellow, brown, red, or blackish spines and are partially hairy or have bristles. The night blossoms are green, white, pink and red.
Care: Easy, especially for grafted specimens. Locate under glass in a warm, sunny and airy spot. Winter rest period temperature should not go below 50°F (10°C). Keep them always humid with calcium-free water. Propagate from seed with subsequent grafting.
Species: *H. albispinus*, up to 15 upright shoots and deep-red blossoms.

H. chosicensis, colorful spines, violet-red blossoms.

H. horrens: dense spines, greenish-white blossoms.

H. pseudomelanostele, branched at the base with golden yellow spines and greenish-white blossoms.

H. versicolor has needles that alternate colors.

Hamatocactus hamatacanthus.

General notes: These attractive cacti from Texas and New Mexico have globular to short cylindrical bodies with deep, often swollen ribs. The middle spines are long, hooklike, and red.
Care: Easy. Locate in a sunny, light, warm place. If its body changes to red, place the plant in the shade. Water regularly, but sparsely. Keep them in the light at 50° to 54°F (10 to 12°C) during the winter rest period. The soil should be nutritious and slightly acidic. Propagate by seed.
Species: *H. hamatacanthus* is dark green. In old age the body elongates. In youth the long, hooklike needles are red; later on they are brownish. *Hamatacanthus* has yellow blossoms with red throats.

H. setispinus has a globular, bluish green body. The ribs are wavy and sinuate. The spines are long and hooklike, even in youth. The large blossoms are greenish yellow on the outside and reddish on the inside.

Harrisia

with *Eriocereus*

Harrisia jusbertii.

General notes: Some plants of this genus are tree-like, shrublike, or climbing. The round, slender shoots have a few ribs and many short spines. *Harrisia* is native to the West Indies and Florida. *Eriocereus* grows in Central and South America. Only older plants of about 3¼ feet (1 m) height flower with whitish, nice-smelling night blossoms.

Care: *Harrisia* is difficult to grow; *Eriocereus* species are relatively easy. These plants need a sunny location, even in winter. During the growth stage, water frequently. The soil should be nutritious and porous. Climbing species need support devices.

Species: *H. jusbertii* (syn. *Eriocereus jusbertii*) does not have many branches. It makes a good base for grafting.

 H. martinii has shoots up to 6½ feet (2 m) long and blossoms up to 8 inches (20 cm) long.

Hatiora

Hatiora salicornioides.

General notes: In their native Brazil, these epiphytic cacti grow on trees or rocks. They have bushy, hanging, main stems and side branches that are arranged like swirls, which are bare or carry short bristles. The limbs are thin at the base; they then thicken in club shapes. The small funnel-shaped blossoms appear out of the crown areoles. They are nice hanging plants.

Care: Relatively easy. They need a warm and light, but not sunny, location. In the summer, they do well outside. It is better to sprinkle or mist them than to water them. During the winter resting period, the temperature should be about 50°F (10°C). Keep them slightly moist. *Hatiora* likes a humous, acidic, nutritious soil, best fertilized organically. In heavy soil, the roots rot.

Species: *H. bambusoides*, blooms orange-red.

 H. cylindrica, orange-yellow blossoms.

 H. herminiae, dark-pink to blue-violet blossoms.

 H. salicornioides, yellow blossoms.

Heliocereus

Heliocereus speciosus.

General notes: These cacti have thin spines and are bushy, climbing, hanging, or epiphytic. *Heliocereus* from Mexico and Guatemala develop very well on the windowsill. The 3- to 5-sided branches in their native habitat are recumbent; in cultivation, they grow upright and need a stick for support.

Care: Relatively easy. In the summer, a wind-protected place outside, with a lot of water, is ideal. For the winter resting period keep them cool and light and keep the soil slightly damp. Provide very nutritious, humous, porous soil. Propagation through cuttings or seeds is not difficult.

Species: *H. speciosus* is the most beautiful of all. It has carmine-red blossoms up to 6 inches (15 cm) long. The cacti grow very rapidly, and are frequently crossed with *Nopalxochia, Epiphyllum, Aporocactus,* and *Selenicereus.*

 H. amecamensis has white blooms. *H. cinnabarinus*, vermilion outside; yellow inside. *H. schrankii* has blood-red blossoms.

Experts suspect that Harrisia jusbertii (syn. Eriocereus jusbertii) is a bastard. That doesn't bother the plant lover. He or she is pleased when enjoying the huge white blossoms, up to 7 inches (18 cm) long.

The sprouts of Hatiora salicornioides are verticilately branched. At the beginning, they are cylindrical or barrel-shaped. Later on they have distinct stems that are up to 1 inch (3 cm) long. Perhaps the prettiest parts are the translucent white top-shaped fruits with their reddish points.

Heliocereus speciosus, the parent of magnificent hybrids, has shiny carmine-red, large blossoms that are also admirable.

EXTRA TIP: At-tention! *Helio-cereus* kept in hanging pots dry out very quickly and should be checked often. Unless you keep them cool during the winter rest period, you will wait in vain for the blessing of flowers.

Hildewintera aureispina

Islaya

Hildewintera aureispina.

Islaya paucispina.

General notes: The only species native to Bolivia, *Hildewintera aureispina* counts as one of the most beautiful of all the cacti. It is probably the most attractive discovery of the cactus collector Ritter in Bolivia. This species, which in its native habitat hangs down from the rocks, branches at the base in a shrublike manner and it is, because of this, an attractive hanging plant. The shoots are only 1 inch (2.5 cm) thick, but they are over 3 feet (1 m) long. The plants have dense, golden yellow spines that look and feel like fur tails. The blossoms grow abundantly and last for several days. They are 2½ inches (6 cm) long and have a double crown. The outer petals are orange-yellow; the middle ones are light vermilion-red with blood-red middle stripes; the inside ones are white to pink. This "miracle blossom" does not exist in any other cactus species and has not been researched biogenetically.

Care: Easy; suitable for beginners. Keep *Hildewintera* under glass in a light, warm and sunny location. In the winter keep them during the day at 59° to 60°F (15° to 20°C); at night, 46° to 54°F (8° to 12°C). Important: The plant must not dry out. Propagation is from cuttings, which root easily. Growing from seed requires a lot of patience. Grafted onto *Harrisia jusbertii*, *Cleistocactus smaragdiflorus* or onto tall column cacti, on the other hand, the plants grow very quickly.

General notes: These globular, short cylindrical cacti with dense, feltlike tufts of hair originate in Peru and Chile. The small yellow blossoms appear in the late summer. The red-haired fruit, filled with air, are characteristic.

Care: Difficult. *Islaya* need plentiful but not full sun. In the summer, warmth and only little water, but mist. In the winter, keep dry and cool; porous and nutritious soil. Propagation from seed is difficult.

Species: *I. bicolor*: purple-green body with yellow, red-sprayed flowers. *I. brevicylindrica*: gray-green; yellowish blossoms. *I. krainziana*: 30 inches (75 cm) long, with reddish-yellow blossoms. *I. paucispina*: blue-green; red-brown spines and yellow flowers.

Lemaireocereus

Lemaireocereus thurberi.

General notes: These cacti grow very tall in their native Mexico, but remain rather small in cultivation. Individual or branched at the base, the body stands upright with dark green shoots and gray spines. The ivory-white blossoms rarely appear in cultivation.

Care: Difficult. Keep the plants, which love the warmth, as close as possible to the glass, and plant them in the earth. They need a lot of room. Water sufficiently in the summer. During the winter rest period keep them light and dry, not below 50°F (10°C). The soil should be nutritious, mineral, porous, and slightly acidic. Propagation is through cuttings or seeds, grafting only with *L. beneckei*.

Species: *L. hollianus* is considered the leading species of this genus.

Leuchtenbergia principis

Prism Cactus

Leuchtenbergia principis.

General notes: There is only one species of cactus in this genus, *L. principis*, the prism cactus. The cactus stands out because of its extraordinary shape. The Agavelike appearance of *L. principis*, which grows between shrubs in northern and central Mexico, puts it in high demand by advanced collectors. On a strong stem with a thick storage root are three-sided, slender, blue-green tubercles that stand spirally and are up to 4¾ inches (12 cm) long. The top areoles are woolly and grey. The yellowish-gray, paper-thin spines are irregularly twisted and up to 6 inches (15 cm) long.

The long, yellow, nice-smelling day blossoms come out above the areoles of the young tubercles. The fruit that develop out of them are spindly, dry, and scaly. The prism cactus remains very small in cultivation and grows very slowly.

Care: Difficult. The location, under glass, should be very sunny. Water evenly and sparsely. Keep it dry during the winter rest period. The soil should be loamy, and very nutritious. Propagation from seed is a very long process; seedling grafting is recommended.

Lemaireocereus thurberi is inclined to cristate form. Although the cactus expert Backeberg allocates them to the genus Marshallocereus, their fruit, which have spines, show the typical characteristics of the genus Lemaireocereus.

Leuchtenbergia principis, the prism cactus, resembles an agave rather than a cactus. The three-sided, long tubercles, trimmed on top, die from the top part down when they get old. The spines resemble threads.

Lobivia

Lobivia tiegeliana looks pectinate; i.e., its spines are arranged like a comb. The crown is sunken. This species blooms abundantly.

Lobivia backebergii grows individually, but also sprouts abundantly. The somewhat slanting, grooved ribs are clearly shown. The spines are partially bent, like hooks.

Lobivia winteriana has a storage root, distinct ribs with oval areoles, and light-brown spines. The ruby-red blossoms have very pointy petals and narrow sepals with green middle stripes.

Lobivia tiegeliana.

Lobivia backebergii.

Lobivia winteriana.

General notes: The name *Lobivia* is an anagram of Bolivia, which along with Peru and Argentina, is the native habitat of these magnificent cacti. They remain small, growing globularly or cylindrically, as individuals or with sprouts.

What makes the *Lobivia* so attractive for the cactus lover are the marvellous, funnel-shaped day blossoms in shiny, bright colors, which can vary even within one species. The splendor covers all shades from red to yellow. Blossoms with strong contrasts, such as red with a green center, pink with a black throat, or copper-orange with a green throat are especially popular.

Care: Easy. *Lobivia* need a light, bright, sunny, and airy location. In the summer they can be outside. Water them a little bit more than other cacti. In midsummer, when the plants bloom, fertilize them regularly. Keep them absolutely dry and cool during the winter. *Lobivia* only bloom when they are kept absolutely dry and at temperatures between 39° and 46°F (4 and 8°C) during the winter. The soil should be very nutritious, only slightly humous, sandy, loamy, and mixed with a lot of pumice stone and perlite. All *Lobivia* are susceptible to red spider mites. Locations with accumulated dry air are dangerous. Propagate through seeds or scions.

Species: *L. arachnacantha*, with yellow-orange blossoms.

L. backebergii, globular, small bodied; blossoms carmine-red with bluish shimmer and white centers.

L. binghamiana, madder-red blossoms with a blue shine.

L. glauca, orange blossoms with a black center.

L. tiegeliana has a globular body and violet-pink blossoms.

L. winteriana, with ruby-red blossoms. See table below for more species.

Other Attractive Lobivia species			
Species	Blossom color	Height in. (cm)	Remarks
Lobivia allegraiana	Silky, blood-red	3 in. (8 cm)	Ribs spirally tubercled
L. emmae	Crimson, scarlet center	4 in. (10 cm)	Narrow, low ribs (about 16)
L. haageana	Light yellow, red center	12 in. (30 cm)	Deeply grooved, slanting ribs
L. hertrichiana	Blazing red to dark-skin color	4 in. (10 cm)	Ribs w. sharp edges, deeply grooved diagonally
L. pentlandii	Orange to carmine	4 in. (10 cm)	Lopsidedly grooved ribs, forms ground cover
L. polaskiana	Egg-yolk yellow, flaming red below	8 in. (20 cm)	—
L. shaferi	Yellow	2¾–6 in. (7–15 cm)	Densely covered with spines
L. vatteri	White, black center	2½ in. (6 cm)	Storage root
L. westii	Orange-pink to gold-orange	8 in. (20 cm)	Straw-colored spines, sprinkled brown
L. wrightiana	Pale lilac pink	6 in. (15 cm)	Storage root; middle spines 2¾ in. (2 cm) long

Lophocereus

Lophocereus schottii.

General notes: These column-shaped and shrublike cacti are by all means suited for cultivation, although they grow up to 10 feet (3 m) tall in their native habitats of Arizona and Mexico, and although only there do they create areoles that are capable of blooming. The small night blooming flowers appear in groups out of one areole in long-bristled flowering zones (precursors of real cephaliums) at the ends of sprouts on older plants.
Care: Relatively easy. Keep them in a very warm location and in bright sun. Water amply. During winter, keep them almost dry and not below 46°F (8°C). The soil should be purely mineral and sandy with some loam mixed in.
Species: *L. schottii* sprouts several yellowish green shoots out of the base. The form f. *mieckleyanus* is monstrous and is especially recommended for cultivation.

Lophophora

Peyote

Lophophora williamsii.

General notes: This cactus, known also by the terms peyote or mescal-button, was known to the Aztecs and neighboring Indian tribes as *peyotl* or *peotl*. It was worshipped as a god that had magical forces. The experts disagree as to whether the genus *Lophophora*, which can be found from Texas to central Mexico, consists of three species or of only one very variable species, *L. williamsii*. *Lophophora* creates individual, sprouting, bluish or yellowish green, soft, flat, globular bodies with strong storage roots. The seedlings are tiny. Older plants have no spines. The ribs are wide, and the areoles carry felt fascicles.
Care: Relatively easy. *Lophophora* grows very slowly. In the summer, keep it in a very warm and sunny spot, which is always somewhat humid. In the winter, keep it cool and dry. The soil must be porous and mineral with a small portion of calcium sulfate. Propagate through seed.
Species: *L. williamsii*, with light pink blossoms.

Machaerocereus eruca

Creeping-devil

Machaerocereus eruca.

General notes: This cactus species from Mexico is closely related to *M. gummosus*, the producer of the pithaya fruit. Its 3-inch-thick (8 cm) shoots, covered with wild spines, creep along the sandy ground. The middle spine points backwards, looks like a dagger, and is 1 inch (3 cm) long. The night blossoms are pure white to pale pink.
Care: Difficult. Locate under glass, in bright sun; at best plant them outside, since they do not take repotting very well. Water only moderately, but mist frequently. The plant is sensitive to wetness. Keep it absolutely dry during the winter rest period, but not below 50°F (10°C). Soil should be porous, nutritious, and slightly acidic. Propagate with cuttings.

Lophocereus schottii does not stand out very much; it does not have a stem and varies considerably in its habitus. The number of the ribs varies between 5 and 9; also, the spines are different on the sterile and fertile shoots.

Lophophora williamsii, the cult plant of the Mexican Indians, is interesting even without its magical background. The spineless cactus with more or less distinct tubercles has dirty-white, brushlike wool bundles at the areoles, which become denser in the sunken crown. At the crown are the small, pale pink blossoms.

Machaerocereus eruca is not incorrectly known as creeping-devil. As a ground cover with spines, it is feared in its native habitat by human beings and by animals.

Machaerocereus is also classified under *Lemaireocereus*.

EXTRA TIP: *Lophophora williamsii* contains the alkaloid mescaline, which causes hallucinations with bad aftereffects, which can result in paralysis or trancelike states.

Mammillaria

Pincushion Cactus

Mammillaria klissingiana at first has a globular body, which later becomes elongated. The small blossoms are pale pink and turn into red fruit, which decorate the plant for months.

For some years, Mammillaria zeilmanniana was the first harbinger of spring in the flower trade. The multiple wreaths of violet-purple blossoms were for many plant lovers the reason they got interested in cacti.

Mammillaria klissingiana.

Mammillaria zeilmanniana.

General notes: Many people recognize the small, globular or cylindrical *Mammillaria*, with their characteristic blossom wreaths. This genus is the most widespread in cultivation. These are the cacti that are offered commercially most frequently in their blooming stage.

There is specialized literature about *Mammillaria* and in many places there are even *Mammillaria* societies, to which lovers of this charming cactus belong. The name stems from the diminutive form of the Latin *mama* and means little wart or tubercle.

The habitat of the *Mammillaria* ranges from the southern United States to Mexico, Guatemala, Honduras, Venezuela, and Colombia. There are over 300 species, growing individually or as a ground cover, and they are extremely varied in shape and spine color. However, all have tubercles (mamilla) that are arranged in an orderly way or in spirals. These overlap, replacing the ribs.

Out of the axils, which are the deepenings between the tubercles from the year before, the blossoms grow in wreathlike shapes, rather than from the crown. The axils are bare in many species, especially in the flowering zone, and covered with woolly hair or with bristles.

The areoles are often covered with felt or wool, especially at the crown. Ring-shaped wool zones in the region of the blossom are typical of some species. The spines are straight, bent or hooklike, fine or coarse, smooth or rough, long or short, jutting out or lying flat, soft or stiff, and hairy or feathered.

The blossoms are large or small and are white, yellow, or red. Even the fruit, which are normally green, are frequently colored coral-red. They decorate the non-blooming plant as well.

Care: Easy. These are wonderful cacti for beginners. *Mammillaria* bloom willingly year after year. The location should be bright, sunny, or partially in the shade. Water rather sparsely. Provide proper drainage. Keep light and dry, rather than cool during the winter

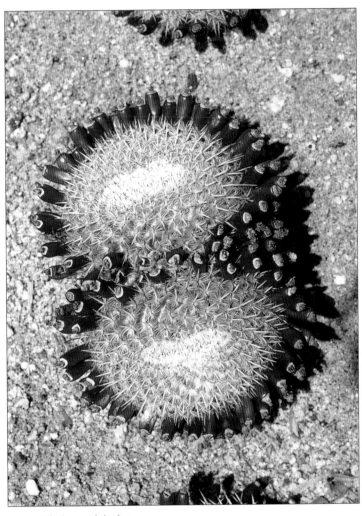

Mammillaria geminispina.

Mammillaria schiedeana.

Mammillaria gemi-
nispina looks quite
dangerous with its
stiff center spines
that grow up to ³/₄-
inch (2 cm) long.

Mammillaria schie-
deana has golden
yellow, raylike edge
spines and white to
yellow axillary wool.
The small blossoms
follow the same color
scheme and barely
stand out.

rest period. A mineral, sandy to gravelly, nutritious soil creates strong, colorful spines and hair. Propagation through sprouts or seeds is easy; some species may be grafted.

Species: *M. albicoma*, small with white, woolly axils and greenish yellow to white blossoms.

M. aurihamata, globular, sprouting; has sulfur-yellow blossoms with red fruit.

M. bocasana forms groups, has whitish hair, yellowish blossoms, and strikingly red fruit.

M. boolii, pink blossoms with greenish stigmata and orange-colored fruit.

M. brauneana has white-woolled, bristled axils, violet blossoms, and carmine-red fruit.

M. densispina is globular and densely covered with spines, with fox-red pointy center spines. Inside, the blossoms are yellow; outside, they are reddish yellow. The plant produces red fruit.

M. elongata has thin, cylindrical, colony-forming bodies, yellow to reddish spines that lie close to the body, whitish yellow blos-

soms, and red fruit.

M. geminispina has large cushions created by the plants' globular or cylindrical bodies, white spines, cream-colored blossoms with a red center, and red fruit.

M. gracilis is a strongly sprouting small plant with white spines that cover the whole body, yellowish white blossoms, and yellowish red fruit.

M. schiedeana is group-forming, and has thick storage roots; it grows whitish blossoms in the fall.

M. zeilmanniana, the best known species, blooms abundantly in wreaths close to the crown. The blossom color is violet to carmine-red, purple, pink, or white. Additional species: *M. herrerae*, *M. insularis*, *M. klissingiana*, *M. kunzeana*, *M. leona*, *M. longiflora* (syn. *Krainzia longiflora*), *M. matudae*, *M. microhelia* (syn. *Leptocladodia microhelia*), *M. mystax*, *M. neocoronaria*, *M. plumosa*, *M. prolifera*, *M. sempervivi*, *M. supertexa*, *M. uncinata*, *M. viereckii*, *M. woodsii.*

EXTRA TIP:
Mammillaria belong to the most willing and most grateful cacti. All species can be recommended for the beginner.

Matucana

with *Submatucana* and *Incaica*

Melocactus

A typical Matucana
blossom has a more
or less zygomorphic
fringe and outer
leaves that are usu-
ally bent back. The
most common color
is vermilion red.

A typical Matucana
blossom has a more
or less zygomorphic
fringe and outer
leaves that are usu-
ally bent back. The
most common color
is vermilion red.

The only species with
a yellow blossom is
Matucana weber-
baueri. The form
flammea is a cultivar
with widespread,
long, yellow-brown
spines all around.

Melocactus maxonii
is a small, wide,
globular Melocactus
with a relatively small
and flat cephalium of
red-brown bristles,
from which the small
pinkish red blossoms
barely stand out.

Closeup of Matucana flower.

Matucana weberbaueri f.
flammea.

Melocactus maxonii.

General notes: In their native Peru, one finds the plants at elevations of 14,625 feet (4,500 m). The flattened globular or cylindrical bodies grow individually with only a few sprouts out of the base. They form cushions very rarely. The ribs are dainty, and the spines are fine or coarse. The day blossoms are red, orange, pink-violet, or yellow; they appear in multiples near the crown. The filaments, styles, and stigmata are vibrantly colored.
Care: Easy. These cacti grow easily and readily bloom. The location should be bright, airy, and sunny. If need be, they can also be partially in the shade. Water moderately in the summer, and fertilize sufficiently. Keep light and cool during the winter rest period. The soil should be slightly acidic and porous.
Species: *M. breviflora*: individual, globular, spines brownish to purple, and carmine-red blossoms.
   M. cereoides: column-shaped with white edge spines, black-sprayed center spines, and red blossoms.

M. comacephala: globular to cylindrical with cream-colored spines that envelop the body; large red blossoms.
   M. crinifera: white blossoms at the bottom; red on top.
   M. haynei: globular to cylindrical with dark spines and scarlet red blossoms.
   M. hystrix: dark carmine-red blossoms with yellow anthers.
   M. multicolor: spines white to black-violet; carmine-red blossoms.
   M. variabilis: white spines; carmine-red blossoms.
   M. weberbaueri: lemon-yellow blossoms.
   M. (Submatucana) paucicostata: up to 6 inches (15 cm) tall; gray, bent spines; dark vermilion, violet-edged blossoms.
   M. (Submatucana) ritteri: up to 6 inches (15 cm) tall; brown, bent spines; vermilion-carmine blossoms.
   Incaica aureiflora: up to 12 inches (30 cm) tall, very coarse yellow to brownish needles; yellow blossoms.

Matucana recently has been classified in *Oreocereus*.

General notes: *Melocactus* are spread all over Central America and Brazil, and they love warmth. The globular, sometimes longish bodies have distinct ribs and are heavily covered with spines. At age 7 years, the plants cease their vegetative growth and form a compact, bristly, felty cephalium, which can be over 3 feet (1 m) tall. The small, reddish blossoms grow out of it.
Care: Very difficult. Keep sunny in warm ground with humid, warm air, in a very large, wide container. Water only a little bit and sprinkle or mist frequently with calcium-free water at room temperature. Do not let the plant dry out entirely in the winter and keep it warm. Acidic, sandy soil is best.
Species: *M. communis*: purple-brown cephalium and dark red blossoms. *M. fortalezensis*: red-bristled cephalium and carmine-red blossoms. *M. glaucescens*: whitish cephalium and red blossoms. *M. maxonii*: brown-bristled cephalium and pink blossoms. It does not need as much warmth.

Monvillea

Monvillea cavendishii.

General notes: These very rewarding column cacti from northern and central South America have many growth forms: upright, low-lying, even climbing. They are willing to bloom and grow quickly and abundantly. Shoots 3 feet (1 m) long have large, whitish-green blossoms, which open up at night.
Care: Easy. *Monvillea* do not need much room. Do not keep them in the full sun. They prefer partial shade and warmth, and soil that is quite moist and humous. During the winter do not let them dry out or get too cold. Propagate with cuttings.
Species: *M. cavendishii*, upright-climbing or bent shoots that have whitish edge spines; white blossoms about 4 inches (10 cm) long.

M. haageana: bluish-green shoots that branch out and short spines; blossoms, greenish-white.

M. spegazzinii: three-sided shoots, white blossoms with purple crown leaves.

Morawetzia

Morawetzia doelziana.

General notes: *Morawetzia* branch out at the base and grow wide and bushy with shoots whose ends swell up like clubs before they start to flower. At the end of the sprout is a woolly and bristly creation, which resembles a cephalium. The yellow to brown spines grow up to 1½ inches (4 cm) long. The bluish red blossoms are up to 4 inches (10 cm) long. The yellow-green fruit are hollow.
Care: Easy. The plants are very willing to bloom, but want to be warm and sunny under glass. At noontime, they should be somewhat in the shade. Keep sufficiently moist. During the winter resting period, keep them almost dry and at 46° to 61°F (8 to 16°C). The soil should be nutritious and slightly acidic. Propagate by seed. Grafting is not necessary.
Species: *M. doelziana*: bluish carmine-red blossoms.

M. sericata: with long, white woolly hair without bristle tufts; vermilion-red blossoms.

Myrtillocactus

Myrtle Cactus

Myrtillocactus geometrizans.

General notes: *Myrtillocactus*, from Mexico and Guatemala, form bushes with upward-bent shoots or (especially at an older age) stems. The shoots are wildly covered with spines, or they have blue rings around them. Up to nine blossoms come out at the same time. Their blossoms, which open in the day, are small and greenish white or reddish white. The blue blueberry-like fruit are edible.
Care: Easy. The cacti, which are recommended for beginners, grow best when they are planted into the ground bed of a sunny, warm greenhouse. The soil should be nutritious and should be kept very moist. Keep the plants dry during the winter resting period, but not under 46°F (8°C). Propagate with cuttings.
Species: *M. geometrizans* (blue candle) in its youth has light blue, wax-covered shoots, reddish edge spines, and a black, daggerlike central spine.

M. schenckii has shoots that stand densely together and have long spines.

Monvillea cavendishii belongs to a genus with 19 species, which are native to Brazil, Venezuela, Ecuador, Peru, Bolivia, Argentina, and Paraguay.

Morawetzia doelziana was thought for a long time to be the only species of the genus. The 4-inch-long (10 cm) bluish carmine-red blossoms with slanting fringes are especially striking.

Myrtillocactus geometrizans has dark red-brown to bluish-purple, sweet-tasting fruit.

Neobuxbaumia

Neobuxbaumia polylopha.

The many ribs are typical of Neobuxbaumia. Depending on the species, there are as many as 50. They are relatively flat and rounded.

The purple-violet or green-yellow to yellowish-pink blossoms of the Neolloydia species open wide, with a diameter of up to 2½ inches (6 cm), often wider than the cylindrical shoots.

All Neoporteria species have more or less carmine-pink blossoms with narrow lancetlike, pointy petals, which only unfold as the flower fades. The Neochilenia species, which are sometimes included in this genus, have white and yellow blossoms.

General notes: These many-ribbed column cacti from Mexico grow individually and are rarely branched. The bat blossoms (in the crown and below), which open at night, are whitish to reddish.

Care: Easy. The location should be sunny and warm. Keep them moderately humid and ensure proper drainage to avoid wet soil. The plants resent a too cool, too humid location. Keep them dry and above 50°F (10°C) during the winter rest period. The soil should be coarse, grainy, calcium-free, very nutritious and porous. Propagate with seed; grafting is superfluous.

Species: *N. mezcalaensis:* yellow spines; greenish-white blossoms, red globe-like fruit.

N. polylopha: up to 50 ribs, long, light spines, red blossoms at old column shoots. *N. scoparia:* giant, branched-out growth with long spines and reddish blossoms. *N. tetetzo:* giant, individually standing, with white blossoms and figlike fruit.

Neolloydia

Neolloydia conoidea.

General notes: *Neolloydia* are globular to short-cylindrical, individual or cushion-shaped cacti from the USA and Mexico. The ribs are divided into tubercles.

Care: Difficult. Only for advanced people. The location should be very hot, in bright sun, and airy, with slight sun protection in midsummer. Water carefully; provide proper drainage to avoid wet soil. They need a dry and cool winter rest period. Soil should be medium heavy, very porous, mineral (a lot of pumice or perlite), and slightly acidic. Only *N. grandiflora* and *N. matehualensis* need a neutral soil. Use flat pots or bowls. Indoors, graft.

Species: *N. ceratites* (purple); *N. conoidea* (purple-violet); *C. cubensis* (yellow-green); *N. grandiflora* (purple-pink with large blossoms); *N. matehualensis* (purple); *N. odorata* (yellowish pink).

> **Under *Neolloydia* one also may find the synonyms *Escobaria*, *Gymnocactus*, *Rapicactus* and *Cumarinia*.**

Neoporteria
with *Neochilenia* and *Chilenia*

Neoporteria villosa.

General notes: The *Neoporteria* described here are widespread in Chile. Sometimes more species are included in this genus. The mostly round or short cylindrical bodies rarely grow taller than 8 inches (20 cm), with distinct ribs and dense spines. The blossoms, close to the crown, are red or carmine pink and appear in the late fall or early winter.

Care: Difficult. In the summer, they need a light and sunny spot with protection from the blazing sun and sufficient water. The winter rest period is a problem because the plants are then very sensitive to wetness. The mineral, sandy soil has to be porous and must have a lot of nutrient salts, one mixed, for example, with brick chips. From October until spring, keep the plants above 50°F (10°C) and leave them alone. Not very well suited for cultivation inside. Propagate by seed.

Species: *N. castanea:* a longish body with notched ribs; areoles at first yellow and feltlike; spines brown-black; fruit greenish pink.

N. gerocephala (syn. *N. se-*

Nopalxochia

nilis, *N. multicolor*) is small and globular with soft, wildly tangled, dense, many-colored spines. The blossoms are 2½ inches long (6 cm) and light carmine.

N. litoralis: columnlike growth; areoles, yellowish, felt-like; spines yellow-white to brown-black; carmine-pink blossoms.

N. nigrihorrida: dark gray-green body; spines at the beginning black, later silver-gray, with light carmine-red blossoms that are white at the bottom.

N. rapifera: short, cylindrical, dark-green body with tubercled ribs; areoles slightly woolly. Spines jut out like a broom and are bent. Pink-red blossoms and globular fruit.

N. subgibbosa: globular body; later up to 39 inches (1 m) or even longer and 4 inches (10 cm) thick. Body at first light, later gray-green. Areoles are large, at first white, woolly. About 24 coarse edge spines and 4 stiff center spines are at first amber-colored; later they turn darker. The 1½-inch-long blossoms are carmine-pink.

N. villosa: cylindrical up to 6 inches (15 cm) tall; light-green, later on dark-violet body; spines light or gray; pink to white blossoms.

N. wagenknechtii: up to 12 inches (30 cm) tall; blackish gray-green body with whitish to light-brown edge spines and dark-brown long center spines. Small light-purple blossoms.

Nopalxochia phyllanthoides.

○ ○ ❗ 🗑 🤲

General notes: These epiphytic cacti from Mexico are distinguished by large, very beautiful day blossoms, and they bloom even twice a year. The hanging, flat shoots, without many leaves, grow up to 39 inches (1 m) long. The strange name stems from the Aztec language and is a combination of *nopal*, or "fig cactus," and *xochitl*, "flower."

Care: Easy. The plants like to be partially in the shade, in the summer under trees. In warm weather, make sure that the root ball is always humid. Keep them light and somewhat humid during the winter; if need be, dry and without frost in the basement. The soil has to be very nutritious and slightly acidic. Hotbed soil or ripe compost with a lot of peat (and perlite) would be suitable. A mixture of calcium sulfate takes care of the necessary calcium. Propagation through cuttings is easy.

Species: *N. phyllanthoides* is the most beautiful kind. The long-stemmed, overhanging shoots are pointed like lancets and are blue-green. The blossoms are 4

Nopalxochia ackermannii.

inches (10 cm) long and pink. On the inside, they are light red to rose red. In the trade, it is called the 'Deutsche Kaiserin' (German Empress).

N. ackermanii comes from Chiapas and Oaxaca in Mexico. It has short shoot stems and pure red blossoms. It was named after the cactus grower Georg Ackermann, who introduced the species in 1824.

The most widespread leaf cacti are hybrids of the two wild forms—*N. ackermannii* and *N. phyllanthoides*. The scarlet red blooming cacti have *N. ackermanii* as a parent. Ones with pink-colored blossoms have *N. phyllanthoides* as a parent.

The two-colored blossoms of Nopalxochia phyllanthoides grow from the upper part of the shoots in each notch. When open they look like water lilies.

The rather loose, widely open, scarlet-red blossoms of Nopalxochia ackermannii are larger than the flat of your hand. The light, long stamens create a pretty contrast.

EXTRA TIP: Hang *Nopalxochia* from the end of May on in a fruit-tree—that becomes it well. But do not forget to water it if it does not rain.

Notocactus
Ball Cactus
with *Brasilicactus, Eriocactus,* and *Malacocarpus* (syn. *Wigginsia*)

Notocactus ottonis var. vencluianus is one of the many variations of the bright green species, with 8 to 12 round ribs. The bent ends of the petals are remarkable.

Notocactus magnificus, also known as Eriocactus magnificus, produces very large, bright yellow blossoms. The narrow edge ribs carry dark, golden yellow spines.

Notocactus ottonis var. vencluianus.

General notes: This very popular genus, which is extremely willing to bloom, is native to Argentina, Uruguay, and Brazil. The plant bodies are globular or cylindrical and sprouting, with many grooved ribs. The spines are very variable, tender or coarse, and of different colors. The numerous large yellow (rarely, reddish) blossoms stand near the top and usually appear during the summer.

Care: Easy. Most of the *Notocactus* are undemanding. They like to be where it is warm and sunny, not in the full sun; if need be, in half-shade. The sandy, humous, slightly acidic, porous soil should be kept damp only in the summer. Wet soil because of poor drainage is damaging. The winter rest period should be dry and cool.

Keep *Brasilicactus* species warmer and sprinkle them, rather than watering. This holds true also for *Eriocactus* species, which have to adjust slowly to the sun in the spring. The fast-growing, abundantly flowering *Malacocarpus* species, on the

Notocactus magnificus.

other hand, need a very nutritious soil.

Propagate by seed. Grafting is not really necessary. Whoever wants to do it anyhow should take *Trichocereus spachianus* or *Harrisia jusbertii* as a base.

Species: *N. apricus* has a light green, globular body and yellowish gray spines, and yellow blossoms with a reddish center. The name indicates that this species grows in sunny spots.

N. buenekeri has a globular, strong, green body, up to 2 inches (5 cm) tall and 2½ inches (6 cm) thick. The

about 20 ribs are divided into short tubercles. The areoles are whitish gray. The white edge spines are tangled on the side and up to 1 inch (23 mm) long. The blossoms shine golden yellow and are 1½ inches (4 cm) long. They are abundantly covered with dark bristles.

EXTRA TIP: *Notocactus* are very suitable for beginners, modest in their needs, and at the same time extremely willing to bloom. There are numerous varieties available.

Notocactus buiningii.

Notocactus leninghausii.

Notocactus horstii.

Notocactus buiningii has up to 16 ribs, which are divided into sharp-edged tubercles. Many cactus lovers know it by the name Malacocarpus buiningii.

As it ages, Notocactus leninghausii (syn. Eriocactus leninghausii) grows more and more columnar, with a slanting top. The blossoms are an inconspicuous yellow-green.

Notocactus horstii, named after the cactus collector Horst, belongs to the rarities of this in generally popular genus; it has silky violet blossoms.

N. *haselbergii* (syn. *Brasilicactus haselbergii*) has a flat, small, globular body covered with light bristle spines. The top turns its many small red to yellow-red blossoms to the light.

N. *herteri* has a globular, somewhat lengthened body, flexible spines on tubercled ribs, and purple-red blossoms.

N. *leninghausii* (syn. *Eriocactus leninghausii*) is globular; later on it becomes like a short column with sprouts at the base. The spines are golden brown and like a tuft of hair at the top. The large blossoms are greenish outside and lemon yellow inside.

N. *ottonis* (with many varieties) has a bright green flattened globular body with a sunken, spineless top. The shiny dark-yellow blossoms have dark-red stigmata.

N. *roseoluteus*: body, copper-green; top, white and woolly; spines, light-brown. The blossoms are bell-shaped, up to 3 inches (8 cm) long, and light salmon-red with a darker center stripe.

N. *rutilans* remains small, only 2 inches (5 cm) tall, with a flat green body and spiral ribs, brown-red spines and pink-carmine blossoms with a cream-yellow throat.

N. *schumannianus* (syn. *Eriocactus schumannianus*) grows on granite and sandstone slag heaps in the rainforests of Paraguay. Its body is densely overgrown with red and yellow shrub lichens—a sign of the high humidity in the air. The cactus' body is wide and round at the beginning, with yellowish to brownish spines and large yellow blossoms. It is rarely and only with difficulty kept in cultivation.

N. *scopa* has a cylindrical, 4-inch-tall (10 cm), fresh-green body, which is completely covered by thin, white edge thorns, and strong center thorns that are reddish, brown-red, brown, or black. It has sulfur-yellow blossoms.

N. *uebelmannianus* creates up to 7-inch-wide (18 cm) flat globes with shiny dark-green tubercled ribs; white, woolly areoles; compressed spines; and very large shiny wine-red to violet-red blossoms.

Other Popular and Easily Obtainable Ball Cactus Species			
Species	Blossom	Plant Height in. (cm)	Remarks
Notocactus (Malacocarpus) buiningii	Large yellow; purple-red stigma	Up to 3 inches (8 cm)	Up to 16 ribs, divided into sharp-edged tubercles
Notocactus concinnus	Canary yellow, 2¾ in. (7 cm) long	2½ in. (6 cm)	Yellow-brown spines
Notocactus floricomus	Yellow	Up to 12 in. (30 cm)	Firm gray spines
Notocactus (Brasilicactus) graessneri	Greenish yellow to light green	Up to 4 in. (10 cm)	Yellow-brown or dark gold-yellow spines
Notocactus (Eriocactus) magnificus	Yellow, very large	Up to 6 in. (15 cm)	Narrow-edged ribs, white or gold spines
Notocactus submammulosus var. pampeanus	Yellow with purple stigma	About 4 in. (10 cm)	Shiny dark-green body; strong spines that stick out
Notocactus tabularis	Shiny yellow	About 3¼ in. (8 cm)	Light, pointy brown spines
Notocactus mammulosus	Canary yellow	Up to 4 in. (10 cm)	18–20 ribs with strong, prominent tubercles

Opuntia

Prickly Pear, Cholla

These fabulous, two-colored blossoms belong to Opuntia azurea, a species that is also remarkable because of its blue-green striped body and blackish spines.

Planted outside all year round in the stone garden, the so-called winter-hardy Opuntia species need locations with mild winters. Together with other succulents, they are an exotic planting alternative.

Opuntia azurea.

General notes: *Opuntia* originally grew from Canada to Argentina. They now grow wild in the Mediterranean area, on the Canary Islands, and in South Africa, Australia, and India. They inhabit coastal deserts as well as snowy regions. Therefore, one can keep species that are winter-hardy, with certain restrictions, outside all year.

The variety of shapes of the *Opuntia*, which sometimes have cylindrical leaves, ranges from dwarf cacti and cushion shapes to shrubs and tree-shaped plants. The segmented sprouts are cylindrical in *Cylindropuntia*, flat and leaf-like in *Platyopuntia*, and globularly divided into cylindrical limbs in *Tephrocactus*.

The mostly tubeless blossoms appear at the sprout edges. Certain species bloom very abundantly and in strong colors. The fruit are often edible; e.g., the cactus figs of *O. ficus-indica*, which belongs to the *Platyopuntia*.

Care: Easy. Species that remain small can be kept un-

Winter-hardy Opuntia in a stone garden.

der glass; larger ones can be placed outside in a very hot and sunny spot in the summer. *Opuntia* need a lot of water, especially the *Cylindropuntia*. Coolness at night is desirable. Keep them in the light during the winter rest period; they should be not too cool and completely dry. The soil should be mineral with a lot of loam and nutrient salts. Heavy fertilizing from time to time is essential. *Opuntia* that remain outside all year need locations facing south, porous ground, with winter protection (of twigs or foil

with holes) from December on. Propagate with cuttings.

Species: Winter-hardy *Opuntia*: *O. rhodantha*: strongly branched; up to 12 inches tall (30 cm); egg-shaped sprouts; blossoms purple-pink, orange, or yellow. *O. vulgaris*: tree- or shrub-like; up to 19½ feet (6 m) tall; thin, shiny fresh-green wide oval sprouts; blossoms sulfur yellow. *O. camanchica*: low; blossoms yellow, orange. *O. polyacantha*: recumbent, branched, bushy; sprouts thin, inverted-egg shape; blossoms yellow, orange.

EXTRA TIP: Careful! The dangerous spines of many species of *Opuntia* are equipped with barbs. The glochids, which easily break off and hook into the skin, are especially unpleasant. Be careful also with the species of *Cylindropuntia*.

Opuntia microdasys.

Opuntia leucotricha.

Opuntia tunicata.

There are many varieties of Opuntia microdasys, the small-bristled Opuntia; among other things, they may be distinguished by the colors of their glochids.

Opuntia leucotricha means "the white-haired Opuntia." When it gets older, the about 3-inch-long (8 cm) spines become soft and elastic and look something like hairs.

Opuntia tunicata not only look dangerous to be near; it's better if you don't come near the thin 2-inch-long (5 cm) white spines.

Opuntia Species and Characteristics			
Species	**Blossom Color**	**Shape**	**Remarks**
Cylindropuntia (Opuntia, Cylindropuntia, Austrocylindropuntia)			
Opuntia (C.) bigelowii	Violet-carmine, yellow, or green yellow with purple spots	Shrublike, up to 3 ft (1 m) tall	Yellowish white spines
Opuntia (C.) imbricata	Purple	Tree-shaped, up to 10 ft (3 m) tall	Brown spines
Opuntia (C.) leptocaulis	Greenish yellow	Shrublike, up to 6½ ft (2 m) tall	Very thin, fresh green sprouts, almost no spines
Opuntia (A.) clavarioides	Yellow-brown	Small; branches like antlers	Tiny spines
Opuntia (A.) verschaffeltii	Strong red	Low; many shoots forming dense lumps	Yellowish, almost bristle-soft spines
Opuntia (A.) subulata	Reddish to red	Stretched out; shrublike; up to 13 ft (4 m) tall	Long, light yellow, broomlike spines
Opuntia (C.) tunicata	Yellow	Low, bushy	Spines reddish and up to 2 in. (5 cm) long
Tephrocactus			
Tephrocactus alexandri	Pinkish white	Globular, divided gray-green body	White spines with dark points
Tephrocactus articulatus var. papyracanthus	Whitish pink	Bushy; longish, round shoots; glochids	Pure white, bandlike spines
Tephrocactus dactyliferus	Orange-yellow	Pillow-shaped	Red, yellow, and brown spines
Tephrocactus floccosus	Yellow or orange	Sprouts about 4 in. (10 cm) long, form high, round cushions up to 6 ft (2 m) in diameter	Sprouts densely covered in white "wool"
Platyopuntia			
Opuntia aurantiaca	Orange	Dense, bushy, 6 to 12 in. (15 to 30 cm) tall	Bristly, thin, dirty-brown spines
Opuntia atrispina	Yellow	Low; shrublike; up to 24 in. (60 cm) tall	Light-green sprouts up to 6 in. (15 cm) wide
Opuntia azurea	Deep yellow with red centers	Short stem, above sprawling branches	Sprouts pale green
Opuntia basilaris	Purple-red	Low; branched upright from base on	Sprouts gray blue-green
Opuntia decumbens	Dark yellow	Low to creeping, about 16 in. (40 cm) tall	Sprouts oval, fine velvetlike
Opuntia elata	Orange	Upright; shrublike; up to 3 ft (1 m) tall	Sprouts deep green, thick, 10 in. (25 cm) long and 6 in. (15 cm) wide
Opuntia humifusa	Sulfur yellow	Creeping	Sprouts dark-green, almost round
Opuntia hystricina	Orange or pink	Recumbent, sprawling	Sprouts round, about 2½ in. (6 cm) in diameter
Opuntia marnierana	Orange-red	Low, bushy	Blue-green sprouts; dark blue glochids
Opuntia microdasys	Pure yellow	Bushy; up to 23½ in. (60 cm) tall	Pale-green sprouts up to 6 in. (15 cm) long; no spines; yellow glochids; numerous shapes
Opuntia microdasys var. rufida	Yellowish	Sprouts distinctly longish, oval	Deep green, brownish glochids

Oreocereus

Oroya

Pachycereus

Oreocereus celsianus.

Oroya neoperuviana.

Pachycereus pringlei.

General notes: These column cacti, densely covered
with hair, are among the
most beautiful *Cereus.* They
grow at elevations up to
13,000 feet (4,000 m) in
South America. They grow
in groups up to 3 feet (1 m)
wide, up to 10 feet (3 m)
tall. *Oreocereus* produces red
to pink blossoms (rarely in
cultivation).
Care: Difficult, can be kept
only under glass, not on the
windowsill. Place them in
the bright sun. During the
day, warm; at night, cool.
Oreocereus need temperature
differences between day and
night! Water moderately,
sprinkle in the evening.
Overwintering dry; at night,
cold, and by day, 50°F
(10°C). Use a nutritious porous soil. Propagate by seed
and grafting of seedlings
and young plants.
Species: *O. celsianus* has
spun areolar hair and long,
yellowish-red spines.
   O. trollii: 20 inches
(50 cm) tall, with fine, completely enveloping hair.
   O. ritteri: snow-white hair.
   O. variocolor: almost no
hair, but has colorful spines.

General notes: Cacti of
this genus grow, as the *Oreocereus* do, in the high
mountains of the Andes. The
globular bodies often sit
deep in the ground. The
spines are very varied in
form and color. The small,
reddish or yellow blossoms
are produced in the crown.
Care: Difficult; only for advanced cactus-growers. Location should be very light
and sunny under glass with
day–night temperature contrasts. The winter resting
period should be very cold
and dry. Soil, consisting of
⅓ each humus, sand, and
loam, should be very po-
rous, nutritious, and moderately damp. Propagate by
seed. Grafting lets the plant
grow faster.
Species: *O. borchersii:* body
enveloped in dense yellow
or fox-red spines; lemon-
yellow blossoms.
   O. peruviana: flattened
globe shape with red
blossoms.

General notes: The giant
column cacti from Mexico
grow rather slowly in cultivation, but they are very attractive even at a young age.
They bloom in their native
habitat with bell-shaped
white or pink day flowers.
Care: Difficult. Needs a
humid and warm location;
water only carefully, and
make sure they have good
drainage. Even during the
winter, keep them relatively
warm and dry. Soil should
be porous, nutritious, and
slightly acidic. Propagate by
seed.
Species: *P. chrysomallus*
(syn. *Mitrocereus fulviceps*)
and *P. pringlei,* with white,
black-sprinkled spines.
   P. marginatus, with areoles
that flow together like
strings of pearls.

Pachycereus **is a synonym for**
Marginatocereus **and**
Mitrocereus.

Parodia

Parodia chrysacanthion.

⬭ ○ 🗑 🦪

General notes: *Parodia* are without doubt among the most beautiful globe cacti of South America. Many of the species, which remain small and grow individually or form groups, were only discovered in the 1920s. Most of them are rather undemanding, and after 3–5 years, they bloom regularly and abundantly. The spines have many shapes and colors. The ribs are arranged spirally and divided into tubercles. The center spines are straight, bent, or hooklike, and often long. The splendid red, orange, or yellow blossoms grow in multiples near the crown and remain open for a couple of days.

Care: Easy; suitable for beginners. Locate those with coarse spines, which need a lot of light, under glass. Those with fine spines also prosper on the windowsill. During their growth period, locate in a sunny and airy place. Water regularly; long dry periods are damaging, as is too much water. Do not spray! Keep them dry and at

Parodia sanguiniflora.

39° to 46°F (4° to 8°C) during the winter rest period. Use a slightly humous, nutritious, and slightly acidic soil with a little bit of sand, perlite or pumice stone for those with fine spines. For those with coarse spines, add more minerals.

Species: *P. aureispina*: small, golden-yellow blossoms.

P. brevihamata: petite, with yellow blossoms.

P. camargensis: 10 inches tall (25 cm), with carmine-red, hairy blossoms.

P. chrysacanthion: wide and globular; blossoms.

P. comarapana: orange-yellow blossoms.

P. comosa: ochre yellow blossoms.

P. faustiana: blossoms are scarlet-red on the outside, yellow on the inside.

P. maassii: short cylindrical with copper-red blossoms.

P. procera: lemon-yellow blossoms.

P. sanguiniflora: shiny, blood-red blossoms.

P. schwebsiana: burgundy to rusty-red blossoms.

P. tilcarensis: bronze to blood-red blossoms.

P. schuetziana: red blossoms.

Parodia chrysacanthion blossoms are real harbingers of spring. But even without blossoms, the wide barrel cacti, covered by bristle-fine, prickly, breakable, golden-yellow spines, are striking beauties.

Parodia sanguiniflora, with gray-brown spines and young white areoles that are like wool felt, pushes entire bundles of blood-red, shiny blossoms out of its crown.

EXTRA TIP: Growing *Parodia* from seed is difficult, because the seeds are extremely small. Through grafting, the growth of the seedlings can be accelerated and the growth of the species that have sensitive roots, like *Parodia nivosa*, *P. brevihamata*, and *P. gigantea*, can be secured.

Pelecyphora

Hatchet Cactus

Pelecyphora aselliformis with its flat, laterally compressed tubercles, on which short spines sit close together like a comb, is a jewel in any cactus collection.

Pereskia (syn. Peireskia), considered the most primitive cactus genus, has, as the species Pereskia aculeata proves, very attractive flowering specimens. Unfortunately, they are not suitable for cultivation indoors.

Pereskia sometimes are offered as potted plants, but they only grow satisfactorily indoors when one has the chance to plant them as rapidly as possible in a greenhouse.

Pelecyphora aselliformis.

General notes: These small, globular cacti from Mexico are shaped like hatchets; they are laterally compressed, with stretched tubercles. The spines are arranged comblike on the longish areoles. The plant bodies sit on a storage-root base deep in the ground and have no recognizable ribs. The blossoms grow at the top.

Care: Difficult; location should be warm and sunny; in the winter, dry and at 50°F (10°C). Soil should be purely mineral, sandy/loamy, and very porous. Grafting is recommended.

Species: *P. aselliformis*: spines shaped like wood lice; blossoms carmine-red.

P. pseudopectinata (syn. *Normanbokea pseudopectinata*): blossoms white to pink.

P. valdeziana: blossoms light-violet.

EXTRA TIP: *Pereskia* are the strangest cacti. They got "stuck" in the course of evolution. On the one hand, they still have leaves like other dicotyledons; on the other hand, they have areoles and spines like the more developed cacti.

Pereskia

Pereskia aculeata.

A potted Pereskia.

General notes: The shrublike, tree-shaped, and climbing *Pereskia* look like deciduous trees. They have wooden branches with leaves that fall off or stay green, but they also have areoles with spines like cacti. Their native habitats are Florida (USA) and tropical America, where some species live in humid, warm rain forests. One may distinguish species with small and large blossoms; some have sweet-smelling blossoms. The species was named after N.C.F. de Peiresc, who lived from 1580 to 1637. (By the way, the genus *Pereskiopsis*, which at first glance looks very similar, does not belong from the viewpoint of biological classification to *Pereskia*; it is—because of its glochids and its large, hard, hairy seeds, and because of its blossom formation—more closely related to the *Opuntia*.)

Care: Easy; undemanding plants for beginners. Planted freely in the greenhouse, *Pereskia* grow and bloom best. They like to be in the sun, or half-shade, in an airy location. In the summer, water them regularly; in the winter, less often. Provide proper drainage to avoid soil wetness. Keep them light and warm during the winter rest period. Nutrients, which should be plentifully given in the soil, are very important. Propagate by seed and branch cuttings.

Species:
Small-blooming shrublike species:

P. aculeata (leafy cactus), with white, pale-yellow, or pink blossoms.

P. diaz-romeroana, P. humboldtii, and *P. vargasii,* with bright red or orange blossoms.

Large-blooming species: [blossoms up to 3 inches (8 cm) across] and large leaves:

P. bahiensis, light carmine-red blossoms.

P. autumnalis (syn. *Rhodocactus autumnalis*), orange blossoms.

P. grandifolia (syn. *Rhodocactus grandifolius*), pink blossoms.

P. saccharosa (syn. *Rhodocactus saccharosa*).

Pfeiffera

Pfeiffera ianthothele.

General notes: *Pfeiffera* are small, bushy plants that grow epiphytically, usually without air roots. The sprouts have thin, bristly spines on a few ribs. The small blossoms come out during the day. The fruit are prickly, berrylike, and edible.

Care: Relatively easy. Locate in a warm place in the summer as well as in the winter, but not entirely in the sun. If the room air is dry, mist often with calcium-free water. *Pfeiffera* species are very sensitive to calcium. Even a neutral pH-factor cannot be tolerated. Acid soil consisting of peat, leaf moss, perlite, compost, and ground charcoal is ideal. Provide plants with a fertilizer containing rather a lot of nitrogen, because of the strong growth of the plants.

Species: *P. erecta:* thin sprouts with white areoles, spines and blossoms.

P. ianthothele: pale green with up to 16-inch-long (40 cm) sprouts. Blossoms, purple-red or pink on the outside; inside, white.

Pilosocereus

syn. *Pilocereus*

Pilosocereus palmeri.

General notes: The species of this large genus, which is widespread in tropical America, are especially in demand because of their bright blue-green or blue-ringed, tree-shaped, or column-shaped bodies. The bell-shaped blossoms, which grow out of woolly areoles of flowering zones (pseudocephalium), open up at night.

Care: Difficult. Only for advanced growers. Locate under glass, where it is sunny and very warm; it is best to plant them directly into the ground bed. Make sure that they get air with high humidity and constant soil moisture in the summer. Soil: porous, slightly acidic. Winter rest period of at least 57° to 68°F (14° to 20°C); at night, not below 50°F (10°C).

Species: *P. maxonii,* blue-ringed, white-haired, with purple-red blossoms.

P. palmeri (syn. *Cephalocereus palmeri,* bluish rings, with wool cap near the crown and densely concentrated areolar wool; blossoms pink to purple.

Rauhocereus riosaniensis

Rauhocereus riosaniensis.

General notes: Of this cactus from Peru there exists only one species, as well as the variety *jaenensis.* The plant body consists of a 39-inch-tall (1 m), thick stem and branches with relatively thick, bluish-green sprouts, which are horizontally grooved. The long spines are at the beginning light-red at the bottom, and yellow on the top; later they all turn white-grey. The white, bell-shaped blossoms are up to 4 inches (10 cm) long and rather densely scaly. They open up at night. The egg-shaped fruit have a raspberry-red color.

Care: Difficult. The location above all must be very warm and light, but not in the full sun. Water moderately. Winter rest period temperature should not go below 54°F (12°C) with low air-humidity. Propagate by seed. Seedlings in the seed bed have to be protected from algae and calcification.

Rauhocereus has to be classified today with Weberbauerocereus.

Pfeiffera ianthothele is a species that is very rarely found in the collection of plant lovers. This is certainly due to the fact that they are so difficult to cultivate.

Pilosocereus palmeri develops its beauty only at an older age. In its youth, it is, as the photo shows, rather plain.

Rauhocereus riosaniensis has strange, funnel-shaped, densely scaly night blossoms with a wheel-shaped fringe.

Rebutia
with *Aylostera* and *Mediolobivia*
Crown Cactus

With Rebutia krainziana, one clearly sees that, as is the case with all Rebutia, the blossoms grow in large numbers from deep within the body.

These small, dainty Rebutia species belong to the most grateful windowsill cacti. Although the individual blossoms don't last very long, one can take delight for several weeks in the large number of buds, which open up gradually one after another.

Rebutia krainziana.

A collection of small Rebutia.

General notes: *Rebutia* got their name from the French wine-grower and cactus gardener Pierre Rebut (1830–1898) from Chazay d'Azergues near Lyon. He received the first specimen of *Rebutia minuscula* from the general practitioner Dr. Weber, who was one of the top cactus experts of the last century. It was later named after Pierre Rebut.

Rebutia are widespread in northern Argentina and in Bolivia; they grow there at a height of 11,500 feet (3,500 m). They are all low, compressed, and globular, with many sprouts growing out of the base. Instead of ribs, the plants frequently have spirally arranged tubercles. The spines are thin and light. The colorful day blossoms are often so numerous that they cover the entire plant.

Today, *Aylostera* species are classified with *Rebutia*. They have more cylindrical bodies, and the style in the blossom grows together with the ovary. *Mediolobivia*, which, as a subspecies, are also classified with *Rebutia*, can be recognized by their

hairy buds, the somewhat larger, hairy blossoms, and bristled ovaries. The more than 15 species are spread out from Bolivia to northern Argentina.

Care: Easy—the optimal beginner's cactus! Locate in an airy and sunny place, in the summer also outside, where the spines will become especially beautiful. *Rebutia* like a high air humidity and, in the summer, an even soil humidity. Keep light, dry, and at 37° to 46°F (3° to 8°C) during the winter rest period. At higher

winter temperatures, they grow fewer buds. Unfortunately, the plants, especially the younger ones, are susceptible to red spider mites. They often take care of their own propagation. The ripe fruit burst, the seeds open up by themselves, and they grow quickly. In addition, the sprouts grow roots easily.

Species: See table on page 73. Whoever wants to collect *Rebutia* will find other species with different blossom colors.

EXTRA TIP: *Rebutia* bloom from a diameter of ⅜-inch (1 cm) on. They are small, colorful, and undemanding, easily taken care of, and just right for the beginner.

Rebutia violaciflora.

Rebutia marsonerii.

The small bodies of Rebutia violaciflora, with golden-brown spines, carry large, light-violet blossoms in the early spring.

Rebutia marsonerii is probably the best-known yellow-blooming species. It has several varieties, among which are some with up to 2-inch-wide (5 cm) blossoms.

Other Beautiful Recommended *Rebutia* Species		
Species	**Blossom Color**	**Remarks**
R. chrysacantha	Brick red	White to yellow spines
R. heliosa	Orange	Light-brown areoles with felt
R. marsoneri	Light to deep golden yellow	Sunken crown; spines often fox-brown
R. minuscula	Pure red	White, thin, bristly spines
R. narvaecense	White to light pink	White spines
R. violaciflora	Light violet	Golden-brown, stiff spines
R. wessneriana	Bright blood-red	White spines up to ¾-inch (2 cm) long
R. xanthocarpa	Carmine red	Glassy, fine spines
R. xanthocarpa var. salmonea	Light salmon	Similar in their growth to R. minuscula
Recommended Beautiful Aylostera *Species*		
R. (A.) albiflora	White with pink center stripe	Brownish spines
R. (A.) deminuta	Cherry red	Smallest species
R. (A.) fiebrigii	Bright yellow-red	White spines
R. (A.) kupperiana	Fiery orange-red	Dark-brown center spines
R. (A.) muscula	Orange	Enveloped by fine, white furlike spines
R. (A.) pseudodeminuta	Dark reddish-purple	Shiny dark-green body
R. (A.) spegazziniana	Dark red	Tiny bristle spines, no center spines
R. (A.) spinosissima	Orange-red	Densely covered with white spines
Recommended Beautiful Mediolobivia *Species*		
R. (M.) aureiflora	Orange-yellow	Yellow-brownish, bristly, fine spines
R. (M.) haagei syn. (M.) pygmaea	Light to dark salmon-flamed	White bristle spines stand like a comb
R. (M.) kesselringiana	Rose red, with light edge and center	Brownish yellow spines
R. (M.) ritteri	Fiery vermilion	

Red blossoms: R. calliantha var. berylloides; R. grandiflora; R. krainziana; R. senilis var. aurescens; R. senilis var. breviseta; R. violaciflora var. knuthiana.
Orange blossoms: R. senilis var. schieliana.
Light red blossoms: R. graciliflora.
Golden yellow blossoms: R. glomeriseta; R. senilis var. kesselringiana and var. sieperdiana.
White to light-pink blossoms: R. xanthocarpa var. violaciflora.
Pink blossoms: R. karusiana.
Violet blossoms: R. senilis var. lilacino-rosea and R. xanthocarpa var. violaciflora.

The white color, extraordinary in *Rebutia*, is produced in hybrid R. hybrida albiflora 'Meisterstuck.' It stems from a cross between a *Rebutia* and a *Pseudolobivia*.

Sulcorebutia, discussed in detail on page 78, are actually a subgenus of the large genus **Rebutia**, with equally attractive and easy-to-care-for species.

Rhipsalidopsis hybrids

Rhipsalidopsis rosea is rarely found as a wild plant anymore. The species has undergone a long cultivation process.

This Easter cactus, with vermilion blossoms, is probably a hybrid of Rhipsalidopsis gaertneri, which takes on a more and more hanging form as it grows older. It therefore is very well suited to a hanging pot.

Rhipsalidopsis rosea.

Rhipsalidopsis gaertneri as a potted plant.

General notes: These plants (among which is the Easter cactus, named because of its flowering time) are hybrids that bloom especially abundantly and colorfully. The small, bushy, epiphytic wild forms come from the tropical rain forests of Brazil. They develop roundish (later, angled) sprouts and notched limbs with areoles that have light bristles. The areoles grow more densely at the tip of the sprout. This is also where the blossoms arise.

Care: Wild sorts are difficult; hybrids, relatively easy. The location throughout the whole year should be light to half-shade and warm. In the summer, the plants can be outside. As soon as the buds are visible, Easter cacti should not be moved or turned anymore, because the altered incidence of light could cause the buds to fall off. Install a light meter! The plant takes temperature shocks just as badly. During the time of growth, from February to October, keep the soil slightly moist with soft water at room temperature. For 4 weeks after the flowering and during the rest period from November to January, water very little. Spray more often. For soil, use fibrous peat or average soil with sand. Propagate through sprout limbs, optimally in May, although it can be done throughout the year. Let the cut surface dry out before you stick it into slightly damp soil.

Species: *R. gaertneri*: body bushy and branched, stem upright; branches later on become hanging. The wide-funnelled, scarlet-red blossoms grow individually or in multiples at the ends of the branches, later becoming light carmine-red berry fruit. This species is widespread in Brazil.

R. rosea has several matte dark-green limbs. Three of the short-tubed pink blossoms usually appear at once. Both of these species are prototypes of the so-called Easter cactus. An assortment of hybrids, sold by the name × *R. graeseri* or Easter cactus, were developed from them. These beautiful specimens, with glossy carmine-red blossoms, grow and bloom especially well.

EXTRA TIP: The formation of blossoms on the Easter cactus only takes place if one keeps the plant at 50°F (10°C) from November to January. Important: Move the Easter cactus as little as possible once the buds have started to appear.

Rhipsalis

Wickerware Cactus

Rhipsalis baccifera.

General notes: These abundantly branched, epi-phytic, climbing or hanging plants originate in the tropi-cal United States and South America, and from Africa to Sri Lanka. The 39-inch-long (1 m) flattened, round, di-vided branches have blos-som areoles with multiple blossoms. The berrylike fruit are very pretty.
Care: Relatively easy. Lo-cate in half-shade; in the summer, outside. The soil must not dry out. Winter rest period: light, relatively warm, and slightly humid. *Rhipsalis* species are very sensitive to calcium. The soil should be porous, slightly humous, with ad-mixtures of charcoal, pumice, and perlite. After strong growth and flower-ing, add fertilizer that con-tains nitrogen. Propagate by seed and cuttings.
Species: *R. baccifera, R. ce-reuscula,* and *R. clavata* have white blossoms. *R. houlle-tiana* has cream-colored blossoms. *R. mesembry-anthemoides* has pink blossoms.

Schlumbergera

with Zygocactus
Christmas Cactus

Schlumbergera 'Golden Charm.'

Schlumbergera truncata.

General notes: The Christmas cacti are the best known and most popular. The bastardizations relate to *S. bridgesii,* but above all to *S. russelliana* and *S. truncata.* The shrublike, epiphytic wild forms originate in the tropical rain forests of Bra-zil. Large numbers of red to white day blossoms appear on divided, leaflike flat branches. The hybrids bloom from December to January; sometimes until March.
Care: Hybrids, relatively easy; wild forms, more diffi-cult. Locate throughout the entire year in light to half-shade where it is warm. The plants love to be outside. Keep them in this "resort" until the end of September. In the summer, keep the soil slightly moist. Until the end of July, fertilize every 14 days with a fertilizer that is low in nitrogen, but con-tains a lot of phosphorus and potash. From August on, greatly reduce water, fer-tilizer, and warmth, so that the leaf limbs ripen and many buds develop. After the buds have developed, increase the amount of water

and the warmth again, but do not fertilize. Optimal temperatures at night are 50° to 57°F (10° to 14°C); daytime, 64°F (18°C). Prop-agation is easy with leaf cuttings.
Species: *S. opuntioides:* a wild form that resembles a *Platyopuntia;* light carmine-red blossoms.
   S. orssichiana has the larg-est blossoms of the genus. They are 3½ inches (9 cm), long, 2¾ inches (7 cm) wide, and are white with light carmine-red borders.
   S. russelliana forms a round, undivided stem with up to 1¼-inch-long (3.5 cm), ¾-inch-wide (2 cm), overhanging light-green branches. The blos-soms, growing at the ends of the branches, are over 2 inch long (5 cm) and dark pink.
   S. truncata (syn. *Zygo-cactus truncatus*) has multiply-divided branches and numerous large bright-pink or deep-violet blos-soms at the end of the branches. The hybrids pro-duce white, pink, red, vio-let, and, more rarely, yellow blossoms.

Rhipsalis baccifera, with extremely thin, hanging branches, is decorated with many little, pearllike berry fruit.

Because of its rare color, one of the most beautiful vari-eties of the Christmas cactus is 'Golden Charm' (a Schlumbergera).

Schlumbergera trun-cata (syn. Zygocactus truncatus) grows in its wild form as a small, bushy shrub. The blossom color is somewhat variable, from pink to dark-violet (see also page 83).

Selenicereus

Night-Blooming Cereus

*Selenicereus grandi-
florus blooms only
once a year, for a sin-
gle night. When the
magnificent, plate-
sized blossom, which
smells of vanilla,
blooms, its owner is
compensated abun-
dantly for many
nights of sleep that
were sacrificed, in or-
der not to miss the
right moment.*

General notes: The stretching, climbing, and creeping *Selenicereus* originate in tropical Central and South America. The plants, which have slender sprouts that branch out, have air roots, low ribs, and short spines, or sometimes no spines at all. They are especially popular because of their huge white night blossoms.

Care: Easy; good for beginners. Locate away from the sun; in the warm regions, keep them outside in the summer in half-shade. Indoors they are best planted directly in the ground bed of a greenhouse. The plants need a strong support device to climb on, such as a grating or sticks. In the summer keep them always slightly moist; in the winter, relatively dry (without their shrinking) and in order to further the growth of blossoms, keep them for some weeks at only 50°F (10°C); not cooler. Use a very nutritious, porous, and slightly acidic soil, with admixtures of peat, loam, compost soil, sand, perlite, and ground charcoal. Propagate by seed and cuttings.

Species: *S. grandiflorus*, the famous queen-of-the-night, produces blossoms that are up to 12 inches long (30 cm) and 8 inches wide (20 cm), which smell of vanilla. They open up only for one night, an event that is always awaited with eager expectation. The buds usually spring open at 10 P.M. with a slight pop, and after that the petals unfold in

Selenicereus grandiflorus.

slow motion. After midnight, the blossoms close up again; the following morning they hang down, faded. The outside sepals on the queen-of-the-night are cream- to salmon-colored; the fruit is edible.

Substances are derived from the blossoms and sprouts of *Selinicereus* that have an effect on the heart; they are used especially in homeopathy. For that purpose, large numbers of branch sprouts are grown in greenhouses. The substances are glycosides that are similar to Digitalis. They occur in all *Selenicereus* species.

S. hamatus (syn. *Cereus rostratus*) creates very long branches and reddish-yellow blossoms.

S. Pteranthus (syn. *C. nycticallus*), the princess-of-the-night, blooms just as magnificently as the queen, but has no scent.

EXTRA TIP: Did you know that substances that strengthen the heart are derived from the queen-of-the-night (*S. grandiflorus*). Its branches contain glycosides that are similar to the ones of the poisonous foxglove (*Digitalis*).

Soehrensia

Soehrensia grandis.

General notes: These strong, round, or short cylindrical cacti, which sometimes are also called giant *Lobivia*, have short-tubed, hairy yellow or red blossoms and woolly fruit.
Care: Easy, suitable for beginners. Locate in an airy place in full sun. As natives of the elevated areas of northwest Argentina and of Chile, *Soehrensia* love strong temperature contrasts between day and night. Water a little bit more than cacti are normally watered, and fertilize frequently. Winter rest period: very cool and dry. Sandy/loamy soil with a high portion of pumice and perlite. Propagate by seed.
Species: *S. bruchii* (syn. *Lobivia bruchii*): multiply-ribbed body; red blossoms.
   S. formosa (syn. *Lobivia formosa*): colorful spines and long, golden-yellow blossoms.
   S. grandis (syn. *Lobivia grandis*): long, orange-yellow blossoms.

Stetsonia coryne

Stetsonia coryne.

General notes: Only one species is known of this treelike cactus from Argentina, Bolivia, and Paraguay: *Stetsonia coryne*. The plants in their native habitat grow up to 26 feet tall (8 m). On thick stems of 16-inch diameter (40 cm) grow numerous thick branches up to 16 inches long (40 cm). The coarse spines are brownish yellow in the beginning; later they become white and, on top of the shoot branch, blackish. The blossoms are 6 inches long (15 cm), tube-shaped, and white to pale pink. They open up very widely at night.
Care: Simple; suited to beginners. *Stetsonia* grows very slowly; it will, therefore, never reach the same height in cultivation as in its natural habitat. The cactus wants to be in the sun. It needs a nutritious, porous, moderately moist, slightly acidic soil and is otherwise completely undemanding.

Strombocactus disciformis

Strombocactus disciformis.

General notes: This cactus resembles weathered pieces of rock. It grows in central Mexico in the clefts of steep limestone and slate boulders. There, it is perfectly adapted to its environment, which it resembles closely. The plant body is a flattened globe with gray-green foliage. The ribs have bulging, leaflike tubercles arranged in spirals. The thorns—except at the crown—fall off. The blossoms are 1½ inches long (4 cm) and yellowish white; they are grouped together in multiples. *Strombocacti* grow very slowly, but they blossom abundantly.
Care: Difficult; only for advanced growers. The plant needs a location in bright sun; it has to be watered very carefully. It needs a cool and dry location in the winter. The soil has to be mineral. Propagate by seed. When grafted, the plant degenerates.

Soehrensia grandis has narrowly edged ribs and remains globular. The funnel-shaped blossoms grow up to 2½ inches long (6 cm) and 1½ inches (4 cm) in diameter.

Stetsonia coryne, the only species of the genus, is highly valued in cultivation, because it grows very slowly. It forms abundantly branched, spread-out shoots. It can look very striking in a bowl.

Strombocactus disciformis resembles a weathered piece of stone in its native habitat. In cultivation, it grows shaped like a disk or a flattened globe. Bristly spines grow mostly on the crown.

Sulcorebutia

The abundantly sprouting Sulcorebutia, completely covered with blossoms, is extremely variable concerning its spines: yellowish, dark-brown, red-brown, and even black-brown spines exist.

Here one can see the areoles, which look like lines, especially well; they are characteristic of Sulcorebutia. The comblike spines, which lie close to the body and cover it, frequently occur in this genus.

Sulcorebutia tiraquensis.

General notes: Because of their many and variously colored blossoms, these globular dwarf cacti from Bolivia are highly valued by cactus lovers. They have pretty spines and often form groups. They distinguish themselves from the *Rebutia* through their coarse spines and long, stretched areoles, which look like lines. The blossoms are funnel-shaped and distinctly scaly.

Care: Easy; beginner's plants. Locate in a very sunny place, but, at the same time, the air should be humid. A greenhouse would be the optimal spot. The soil should be kept damp during the summer. During the winter rest period, on the other hand, *Sulcorebutia* should be kept absolutely dry and very cool. The plants love nutritious, purely mineral, loosened soil. Grow them from seed or cuttings. Grafting is not recommended. *Sulcorebutia* are susceptible to red spider mites.

Red-blooming Sulcorebutia.

Species: *S. krahnii*: spirally tubercled; yellow blossoms with white throat.

S. lepida: vermilion to carmine-red blossoms.

S. mentosa: purple-colored blossoms.

S. rauschii: black-green to violet, only a few centimetres tall (1 inch) plant body; magenta-pink blossoms.

S. steinbachii: cushion-forming; blossoms, laterally in the center of the body, are scarlet- to violet-red.

S. tarabucensis: dark-red blossoms with yellow throat.

S. tiraquensis: purple blossoms, violet-pink fruit.

S. totorensis: purple blossoms.

S. tunariensis: deep red blossoms.

S. vasqueziana: dark plant body; dishevelled, tangled spines; white feltlike areoles; blossoms magenta-red, yellow inside.

Sulcorebutia **is classified with** *Rebutia*.

Thelocactus

Thelocactus and Coryphantha.

○ ○ 🌡 ⧠ ⍩

General notes: The globular or stretched *Thelocacti*, called "thelos" for short, which come from Mexico or Texas, grow about 8 inches tall (20 cm). The ribs are tubercled; the areoles are long-stretched. The coarse, strikingly colorful spines are especially attractive. Thelos bloom in summer with very large, bell-shaped day blossoms.
Care: Difficult; only for experienced people. The location should be very sunny, warm, and airy; the windowsill, therefore, is not the right spot. Water carefully; ensure proper drainage to avoid wet soil. In the winter, the thelos want to be completely dry and at always the same temperature: 46° to 50°F (8° to 10°C). The purely mineral soil should be very porous and nutritious. Grow from seed. Grafted plants have a loss of growth and loss of intensity of the spine colors.

Species: See table. Other attractive *Thelocacti* are:

T. bueckii: reddish; spines that are bent back or outwards; dark carmine-red blossoms.

T. conothelos: white spines, purple-violet blossoms.

T. ehrenbergii: dark spines, carmine-pink to white blossoms.

T. flavispinus: yellowish spines, purple-pink blossoms.

T. hastifer, white to horn-colored spines, pale violet-pink blossoms.

T. heterochromus: large white areoles; reddish or brownish, light-speckled or banded spines; light violet blossoms.

T. hexaedrophorus: yellowish, gray-pink or brown-red spines; white blossoms.

T. leucanthus: gray spines, yellow blossoms.

T. lloydii: yellowish spines with red tips; pale-purple blossoms.

T. nidulans: body is a wide, flattened globe, up to 8 inches tall (20 cm); thorns in old age shiny gray-white; blossoms, greenish white.

T. wagnerianus: yellow or red spines; red blossoms.

Thelocactus and Coryphantha, neatly arranged. The tubercles of Thelocactus flow together into ribs with somewhat longish areoles.

Other Well-Known Thelocactus Species			
Species	**Blossom Color**	**Plant Height, Inches (cm)**	**Spine Color**
T. bicolor	Deep purple-pink	Up to 8 in. (20 cm)	Yellowish to red
T. lophothele	Yellowish-white, sulfur yellow, peach-colored/rose-red, and silver-shiny	Up to 8 in. (20 cm)	Black to light brown; upper spines ruby-red
T. tulensis	Silver white to pale pink	Up to 4¾ in. (12 cm)	Whitish with dark tip
T. schwarzii	Reddish-purple, scarlet towards center	Up to 2½ in. (6 cm)	Yellowish

Trichocereus

with Helianthocereus

Trichocereus chilensis sometimes is shrub-like and sometimes treelike in its native habitat, where it grows up to 9¾ feet (3 m) tall. It is the host plant of a small mistletoe (Phrygilanthus aphyllus), which decorates the cactus with bright red blossoms and berries.

Trichocereus pasacanus, also known as Helianthocereus pasacanus, is a characteristic plant of the Puna, a high plateau region of Bolivia and Argentina. Its habitus strongly resembles Carnegia gigantea.

Trichocereus chilensis.

General notes: *Trichocereus* are native to southern and central Argentina, Ecuador, Peru, and Chile, where they grow from the coast to the high mountains of the Andes. There are numerous growth forms. Besides the ones that grow to be 3 feet (1 m) tall, there are species that are recumbent and ones that form cushion shapes. The spines are also very variable. Some are extremely long and strong. The giant blossoms of the *Trichocereus* open up at night. They are long and funnel-shaped, densely woolly, and mostly white. The day-blooming species were formerly grouped under the name of *Helianthocereus*, but now they are referred to *Trichocereus* again. The bright, short-funnelled blossoms are typically white, yellow, or red. In cultivation, *Trichocereus pachanoi*, an almost spineless species, and *T. spachianus*, are above all vital bases for grafting. The wood of the magnificent *Trichocereus pasacanus*, which grows up to 33 feet (10 m) tall in very thick columns or sparsely branched

Trichocereus pasacanus.

trees (a little bit like *Carnegia gigantea*), is used in Argentina to build fencing, as firewood, or for the production of souvenirs.

Care: Easy. The location should be sunny. In the summer, water evenly and, because of the strong growth, fertilize again and again. In the winter, place the plant in a cool and completely dry location. A normal, slightly acidic cactus soil is sufficient. Growth is by seed or cuttings. Older plants have to be tied or supported.

Species: *Trichocereus bridgesii*, up to 16¼ feet (5 m) tall, with 7-inch-long (18 cm) blossoms.

T. camarguensis: up to 20 inches tall (50 cm); 8-inch-long (20 cm) blossoms.

T. candicans: up to 30 inches tall (75 cm); forms colonies; blossoms, up to 8 inches long (20 cm), have a strong scent.

T. chilensis: 10-foot-tall (3 m) columns.

T. courantii: up to 14 inches tall (35 cm); blossoms, 9½ inches long (24 cm), wonderfully like roses.

T. fulvilans: grows up to 5 feet (1.5 m) tall; nice-smelling blossoms.

T. glaucus: 3 to 6½ feet tall (1 to 2 m); blossoms about 6 inches (15 cm) long.

EXTRA TIP: *Trichocereus* **are among the most vital and at the same time the most undemanding cacti, and they prosper even if one hardly ever takes care of them.**

Helianthocereus poco.

The purple-colored blossoms of Helianthocereus poco catch the eye, just as the spectacular spines do.

Helianthocereus 'Vogesen' is a pretty variety with attractive carmine-pink blossoms.

Helianthocereus 'Vogesen.'

T. macrogonus: 6½ feet tall (2 m); the sprouts have rings.

T. pachanoi: tree-shaped; does not form spines in cultivation.

T. schickendantzii: 10 inches (25 cm) tall; blossoms up to 8¾ inches long (22 cm).

T. spachianus: huge blossoms in the crown. For additional species, see table.

Additional Helianthocereus Species			
Species	**Blossom Color**	**Plant Height**	**Remarks**
Shrublike Species of Helianthocereus with Slender Shoots			
H. crassicaulis	Fire-red	Up to 6½ in. (16 cm)	Body at first globular
H. grandiflorus	Bright red	Up to 14 in. (35 cm)	Body deep green
H. huascha	Golden yellow	Up to 20 in. (50 cm) or more	About 17 ribs
H. pecheretianus	Blood red	Up to 18 in. (45 cm)	15–20 ribs
Species of Helianthocereus with Thick Shoots			
H. antezanae	Light yellow	Up to 8 ft. (2.5 m)	Up to 4-in.-long (10 cm) thin, pale-yellow spines, tangled in the crown
H. atacamensis	White	Up to 20 ft. (6 cm) or more	Mostly without branches
H. bertramianus	Yellowish cream white	Up to 6½ ft. (2 m)	Whitish spines
H. conaconensis	Cream-colored	Up to 6½ ft. (2 m)	Bristly, up to 6-in.-long (15 cm) spines
H. escayachensis	White	Up to 13 ft. (4 m)	Grey, broomlike spines
H. herzogianus	Cream white	Up to 7 ft. (2.2 m)	Club-shaped, deep-green shoots
H. narvaecensis	White	Up to 3 ft. (1 m)	Shiny, dark-green shoots
H. orurensis	Light purple or purple-pink	Up to 6 ft. (1.8 m)	Brown-yellow spines
H. poco	Light purple-pink	Over 5 ft. (1.5 m)	Light brownish, partially dark-striped spines
H. randallii	Deep purple	Up to 3 ft. (1 m)	Body cylinder-shaped
H. tarijensis	Light wine-red	Up to 5 ft. (1.5 m)	Somewhat smaller blossoms

Turbinicarpus

Uebelmannia

Wilcoxia

Turbinicarpus klinkerianus.

Uebelmannia pectinifera.

Wilcoxia viperina.

General notes: These very small barrel cacti from Mexico have soft, bent spines that often only appear on the crown. The blossoms are shaped like slender tubes. Although *Turbinicarpus* species grow fairly well ungrafted, they are often grafted to bloom more abundantly. However, grafted plants degenerate.
Care: Difficult; only for experienced people. Location should be airy, light, but not in the full sun. Water in the summer very carefully; provide proper drainage to avoid wet soil. Keep dry, cool, and light during the winter rest period. In the summer, there is a growth pause. The dwarf cacti stand ungrafted in porous, mineral soil that is mixed with some loam and calcium sulfate.
Species: *T. gracilis*: white blossoms with a pink center stripe.
T. klinkerianus: pure white blossoms.
T. lophophoroides: white woolly blossoms on top, with a touch of pink.
T. schmiedickeanus: pink blossoms with a violet center stripe.

General notes: This cactus genus was discovered only in 1966. Until now, it has only been found in northern Brazil, and it is special. In most of the few species, the spines stand up like a comb. The plants only grow 20 inches (50 cm) tall.
Care: Difficult. *Uebelmannia* are only recommended for experienced collectors. They want to be in a sunny and warm spot, at best directly under glass, and they want to be sprinkled several times a day on sunny winter days. During the winter, keep them not entirely dry at 50°F (10°C). The soil should be mineral, acidic, porous, and mixed with leaf mould. Grafting is recommended.
Species: *U. buiningii*: Ribs dissolved in tubercles; yellow blossoms.
U. flavispina: comb-shaped spines; light yellow blossoms.
U. gummifera: sulfur-yellow blossoms.
U. pectinifera: globular with a waxlike coating; greenish yellow blossoms.
U. meninensis: yellow blossoms.

General notes: These dwarf, shrublike cacti bloom very beautifully and willingly, especially when grafted. This is preferable to propagating with cuttings, and it is recommended, because seedling plants grow very slowly ungrafted and because the huge storage roots are very difficult to fit into a pot later on. The spines of the *Wilcoxia* are short, fine, and hairy or bristly. The large white or red funnel-shaped day blossoms grow near the crown.
Care: Relatively easy. Grafted plants do not cause any problems; they can even stand in half-shade. Ungrafted specimens need sun and porous, very meager soil. During winter rest period, keep them dry at 50 to 54°F (10 to 12°C). In the spring, water only when their blossom buds have clearly developed.
Species: *W. albiflora* (white blossoms); *W. poselgeri* and *W. viperina* (purple).

Hybrid of Zygocactus truncatus (syn. Schlumbergera truncata).

The Most Beautiful Succulents and Their Care

How much room do you need to bring the exotic world of the other succulents into your house? You do not need much. A windowsill is enough to accommodate everything you see here: the bizarrely wound aloe with its dangerously toothed leaves; the short-stemmed *Cotyledon undulata*, whose leaves are covered with a touch of red; the dainty rosettes and very pointy leaves of a second aloe; a small cushion of sedum, whose short, cylindrical, thick little leaves turn fiery red in the sun; a wide *Echeveria* rosette; and the bushy *Kalanchoe*, whose leaves are so prettily colored red at the edges. There are thousands of ways to put together such mini-landscapes from the wide variety of succulent shapes and colors.

A colorful grouping of succulents.

Adenium obesum

Desert Rose

The large, funnel-shaped blossoms of the desert rose, Adenium obesum, stand as many as ten together in cymes; the blossoms have a cylindrical base; the petal tips are pink, large and wide.

Here one clearly sees the difference between an Adenium obesum that is grafted onto an oleander and a wild form. The cultivated plant grows more compactly and blooms much more abundantly.

Adenium obesum.

General notes: The wild form, which has a lot of shapes and is a stem succulent originating in the dry regions of Africa, is rarely cultivated because it grows very slowly and does not bloom nicely. It belongs to the dogbane family (Apocynaceae). It is easier to take care of it when it is grafted onto *Oleander*, with its branched stem and thick, spineless branches. Then it blooms in early summer and again in late summer. The blossoms are magnificently red to light pink and last up to 2 weeks. The narrow, dark-green little leaves do not stand out.

Care: Easy; suitable for beginners. The desert rose wants to be where it is very light and fully in the sun. It is the ideal winter plant for indoors, because it does not mind dry, warm air at all. The more it is in the sun, the more abundantly it blooms. If, during the winter, it remains in a warm room, it continues to grow. If it is placed where it is cool, it takes a winter break and sheds its leaves. If the plant is on the windowsill, it should be turned regularly, otherwise it grows in only one direction—i.e., towards the light. In the summer, water it a lot, but provide proper drainage to avoid wet soil. During the winter, the amount of water depends on the temperature. If the plant stays where it is cool, water less. From March to September, fertilize every three weeks with cactus fertilizer. Grafted plants do fine in normal flower soil, ungrafted ones need a dirt-and-sand mixture. Repot them between the first and second bloom-

Adenium obesum: left, grafted on an Oleander; right, not grafted.

ing periods. If the plants grow too large, the shoots can be shortened to half their size between the two blooming periods. The side shoots of the *Oleander* have to be cut off. Propagation is by cuttings or seeds, or air laying. Careful! All parts of the plant are poisonous.

Species: The most frequently seen one is *A. obesum*, which, in its natural habitat, blooms very strikingly during the dry period. Whether the other species are only varieties has not been clarified.

Adromischus

Adromiscus maculatus.

General notes: These dwarf, shrublike leaf succulents from the Crassulaceae family originate in south and southwest Africa. They have round or club-shaped thick, fleshy leaves with smooth or wavy edges on a short stem. They are bare, sometimes hairy or very nicely patterned. Their very tangled air roots grow out of the stem. The blossoms are small, whitish to reddish, and not prominent.
Care: Easy and undemanding; suitable for beginners. Only in a light, sunny, warm location will the leaf patterns develop completely. In the summer, water abundantly; in the winter, hardly at all. The plants cannot tolerate temperatures below 50°F (10°C). Use a porous and humous soil. Propagate with leaves that have fallen off.
Species: *A. festivus:* blue-green to chalk-white leaves with purple speckles.
A. maculatus: egg-shaped leaves with hornlike edges and red patterns.

Aeonium

Aeonium arboreum 'Schwarzkopf.'

General notes: There are over 30 species of these Crassulaceae, which are native to the Canary Islands, Madeira, North Africa, and the Mediterranean. The stemless leaf rosettes either lie on the ground or form the ends of not very ramified branches of small shrubs. After the blossoms fade, the entire plant—or the branch that carries the blossoms—dies. The blossoms are yellow, rarely white or reddish.
Care: Easy. The plants like to be in a light location; in the summer, in half-shade outside, but they have to be protected from the full sun. They do not survive temperatures below 50°F (10°C). Water and fertilize a lot during the flowering time, but not during the growth pause in mid-summer. The soil should be made of sand and humus. Put the plants into pots that are too large rather than too small. Species with solitary rosettes can be propagated only by seed; those that form shrubs can also be propagated through head or leaf cuttings.

Aeonium tabuliforme.

Species: Often very hybridized.
   A. arboreum is 3 feet (1 m) tall. It has flattened rosettes made of leaves with white cilia; the leaves grow on stems that are sparsely branched. The blossoms are golden yellow. The mutations cv. *atropurpureum*, with purple leaves, cv. *albovariegatum*, with white leaves, and cv. *luteovariegatum*, with yellow-white striped leaves are very nice.
   A. canariense has pale green blossoms.
   A. haworthii forms bushes that have a lot of branches with rosettes that lie very close together.
   A. lindleyi has fine, hairy leaves.
   A. nobile grows very large and has fantastic orange-red blossoms.
   A. tabuliforme, the best-known species, has flat, plate-shaped, grass-green rosettes up to 20 inches wide (50 cm). The narrow rosette leaves are spirally arranged and lie above each other like roof tiles. The inflorescence grows up to 24 inches (60 cm) tall and has numerous sulfur-yellow blossoms.

Adromischus maculatus (syn. Cotyledon maculatus) has an elongated peduncle with numerous slightly wavy, shiny green leaves with hornlike edges.

Aeonium arboreum cv. 'Schwarzkopf' is certainly a very attractive Aeonium arboreum variety. The shiny dark red-brown leaf rosettes hardly ever turn green, even in winter at a lower intensity of light.

The flat-sitting, plate-shaped rosettes of Aeonium tabuliforme grow up to 20 inches (50 cm) tall. After the plants bloom, they die.

Agave

Agave parryi.

General notes: Agaves, from the family Agavaceae, have sword- or lancet-shaped hard leaves that are sometimes pointy like needles, toothed at the edges, and often blue-green ringed, arranged in basal, branchless rosettes. The fascinating, 39 inch-tall (1 m) panicles, with thousands of blossoms, can be only seen in their native habitats: the southern United States, Mexico, Central America, and the Mediterranean region. After flowering, the plants die, but they create runners.

Care: Relatively easy; needs a very sunny and airy location; in the summer can be a tub plant outside. During the growth period, water and fertilize abundantly. The soil should contain loam and be nutritious and porous. There should be no water in the funnels of the rosettes. Winter rest period, dry, but not below 41°F (5°C). Propagate by seed, plantlets, or runner rosettes.

Species: *A. americana* can be found in the Mediterranean countries, often growing wild in many varieties.

Agave americana 'Marginata' on a stone cliff.

Leaves jut out stiffly, hanging over in the upper part.

A. attenuata has rosettes of 6 to 15 leaves on a stem up to 3 feet (1 m) tall. The wide green, spineless leaves with white rings are up to 28 inches long (70 cm).

A. filifera: small, globular rosettes with numerous matte-green leaves that have white lines and light, horn-like edges. Var. *compacta* is even smaller and is suitable for a windowsill.

A. parryi: almost winter-hardy; stemless rosettes; stiff, wide, smooth gray leaves with straight end thorns.

A. parviflora: one of the most beautiful species that remains small. It forms small rosettes out of narrow, dark-green leaves with white lines.

A. sisalana: source of sisal hemp.

A. utahensis has large stemless rosettes, with light- to blue-green leaves and end thorns that are up to 3 inches long (8 cm).

A. victoriae-reginae grows slowly. The half-globular rosettes have stiff, white-striped leaves.

Aloe

Aloe ferox.

Aloe arborescens 'Variegata.'

General notes: Aloes belong to the family Liliaceae and originated in Africa, Madagascar, and the Mediterranean area. There are very diverse growth forms. Most species have stemless rosettes that grow in groups. The blossoms are red, yellow, and rarely, white, often on high inflorescences.

Care: Easy. Sunny location; larger, more robust species can be in tubs outside during the summer. Do not water too much; during the winter rest period, keep them dry. Slowly get the plants accustomed to the sun in the spring. Some turn red in the bright sun. In a nutritious soil with humus, they bloom rapidly. They are susceptible to mealy bugs, especially in the winter.

Species: *A. albiflora* has pure white blossoms.

A. arborescens has juices that help alleviate burns. Sword-shaped, gray-green leaves in rosettes on a stem; leaf edges with pointy teeth; red blossoms.

A. aristata: winter-hardy; stemless rosettes with over 100 lancet-shaped leaves; leaf edges hornlike and white-toothed; orange-red blossoms with up to 20-inch-tall (50 cm) inflorescences. Remains small.

A. barbadensis (syn. *A. vera*) has thick, gray-green leaves at the beginning; speckled, stemless rosettes or ones with very short stems; densely covered with yellow blossoms.

A. brevifolia is a strongly sprouting, dwarf species with short-stemmed rosettes of triangular leaves with sharp teeth.

A. ciliaris has long, creeping, climbing stems; blooms very willingly.

A. ferox: many varieties.

A. haworthioides: rosette very small, sprouting; leaves with white pustules and white, dentate edges.

A. humilis forms a ground cover; rosette leaves have various forms and colors.

A. striata has bluish-white leaves with red edges.

A. variegata (tiger aloe) has leaves that are arranged like roof tiles with irregular white bands.

A. albida, A. descoingsii, A. minima, and *A. parviflora* are recommended dwarfs and rarities.

EXTRA TIP: Since the Middle Ages, aloe has been used in remedies and fumigating agents. In the beer-brewing business aloes served from time to time as a substitute for hops. Today, aloe is used in the cosmetics industry. *Aloe vera* provides the active ingredient for many cosmetics.

Anacampseros

Argyroderma

Bowiea

Anacampseros papyracea.

Argyroderma pearsonii.

Bowiea volubilis.

Most of the time, the short stems of Anacampseros papyracea have low-lying, little branches, 2 to 2½ inches (5 to 6 cm) long and ⅓ inch (9 mm) thick. The blossoms are greenish white.

In Argyroderma pearsonii, the cleft between the half-globular leaves is deep, but relatively narrow. The plants usually grow without branches above the ground.

Bowiea volubilis is a curiosity. The bulb is planted above ground. It turns green and produces a leaf that resembles a blade of grass. Every year, the plant grows a long, twin sprout with side branches and blossoms.

General notes: *Anacampseros* belong to the Portulaceae family. They are native to south and southwest Africa. The "white" species are especially popular: low bushes, thickened at the stem and at the roots, on which spirally arranged, small green leaves are totally enveloped by silver-white side leaves. Other species have fleshy leaves, cobweblike hair felt, and side leaves that are transformed into hair. The blossoms are white or reddish.
Care: In the case of stem-succulent species, locate in a very sunny and warm spot; water very little. Adhere to an absolute rest period in the winter. Use sandy, porous soil with loam. Propagate by seed or cuttings. Leaf-succulent species are easier to care for.
Species: *A. filamentosa:* small, thick, rounded red leaves. *A. papyracea:* the most beautiful "white" species; difficult. *A. telephiastrum:* up to 2 inches tall (5 cm).

General notes: These silver-skinned members of the carpetweed family (Aizoaceae) can be only found, highly adapted, on the quartz fields of the Cape Region (South Africa). The stemless plants, only a few centimeters tall (1 inch), which grow by themselves or in agglomerations, consist of two smooth, half-egg-shaped or finger-shaped, backwards bent, silver-gray to olive-green leaves, which grow together at the base. The pretty blossoms are red, yellow, or purple.
Care: Difficult. Location should be very sunny; during the vegetative time from May to October, water only as much as is needed to keep the leaves from fading. If one waters too much, the plants burst or get brown spots. Use sandy soil with a clay or loam admixture. In the winter keep them dry, light, and above 59°F (15°C).
Species: *A. blandum* (blossoms purple-red); *A. brevipes* (light-red); *A. octophyllum* (yellow); *A. schlechteri* (purple with white).

General notes: These Liliaceae from Africa grow out of globular green bulbs that are up to 8 inches thick (20 cm); the bulb remains above ground. The long, thin stems twine and wind very high; in the early spring, the short-lived leaves appear. The white or yellow blossoms are greenish at the edge, and stand in panicles on a climbing stem. After the growing time, the stems dry up.
Care: Place in the greenhouse or in the bright window of a cool room. During the growth and flowering periods, water moderately. After the sprouts have died, place the bulb in a dry, cool spot; after January, it will sprout again. The soil should be loamy; the pots should not be much larger than the bulbs. Replant only every couple of years. In the ground bed of a greenhouse, leave the bulbs in one spot. Otherwise, propagate by seed.
Species: *B. kilimandscharica* (yellow blossoms) and the similar *B. volubilis* (green-white) build large clumps.

Caralluma

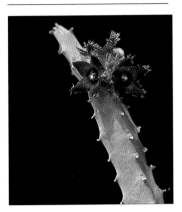

Caralluma joannis.

General notes: This stem succulent genus from the milkweed family grows from South Africa to India. The dentate sprouts have 4 to 6 sides, are basally branched and grow like ground cover; more rarely, they creep or grow upright. The decorative blossoms smell like a carcass.
Care: Easy; suitable for beginners. Place in a warm location, not below 50°F (10°C). Avoid the full sun. In the summer, water moderately from below. Provide good drainage. Keep dry during the winter. The soil should be very porous, sandy, and somewhat humous. Propagate through side sprouts and seeds, which sprout very fast. Susceptible to mycosis (black rot), mealy bugs, and scales.
Species: *C. armata:* greenish, red-speckled blossoms. *C. dummeri:* olive-green hairy white blossoms. *C. europaea:* blossoms greenish yellow with red-brown stripes. *C. joannis:* blossoms in bundles, olive to purple.

Cephalophyllum

White-blooming Cephalophyllum.

General notes: The native habitat of these shrublike or stemless members of the Aizoaceae is South Africa. They are branched, remain low, and form mats. The three-sided leaves are for the most part arranged like tufts of hair. The very large yellow, red, or white blossoms open up only in the afternoon.
Care: In the summer, place outside in a very sunny spot; in the winter, keep them cold and dry; use meager, porous soil. Propagate by seed or cuttings.
Species: *C. alstonii* has almost cylindrical, about 2¾-inch-long (7 cm) gray-green dotted leaves with tufts of hair. The 2 to 3-inch wide (5–8 cm) blossoms are dark red.
    C. subulatoides: lightly dotted leaves and purple blossoms.

Ceropegia

Ceropegia russeliana.

General notes: *Ceropegia* are members of the Asclepiadaceae (milkweed family). Some are root succulents; some are pendant or climbing plants; some are partially upright stem succulents. They are native to South Africa, Asia, and Madagascar. The blossoms are very varied; some have grown-together corolla lobes that form lanternlike structures; some have hairlike barriers that temporarily lock pollinating insects into a trap; and some have tubular corollas that are widened like a lantern or parachute.
Care: Easy. Location should be bright (for stem-succulents) or partially in the shade (for root-succulents); temperature never below 54°F (12°C). Soil: sandy–loamy, containing humus. Water moderately in the summer; in the winter, barely water. The drier the cultivation, the more prominent is the color contrast of the leaves.
Species: *C. haygarthii* and *C. sandersonii* are twining plants. *C. woodii* is a hanging plant; it looks especially beautiful in hanging pots.

Caralluma joannis looks rather pretty with up to 4-inch-long (10 cm), 4-sided branches that have small dents. The olive-yellow and red speckled purple-colored blossoms appear in groups of 2 to 10.

Cephalophyllum species are collector's items. The nicest ones often can only be induced to bloom with additional lighting. This white-blooming species is one of the lesser-known specimens.

Ceropegia russeliana shows the bizarre shape of the trap blossom, which is characteristic of the Ceropegia. Its pretty pattern is supposed to lure insects.

Conophytum

General notes: The genus *Conophytum* belongs to the carpetweed family (Aizoaceae) and includes over 300 species, originally from Africa. The dwarf plants, which branch out a lot when they grow old, form mats or cushions. Only two highly succulent leaves are produced on the sprouts per year. The two leaves are united except for a small cleft between them. They form a globe or have free leaf tips. The white, yellow, or reddish blossom grows out of the cleft. The little plant bodies are globular, egg-, or heart-shaped; at the tip they may be flat, dentate, notched, dotted, tubercled, or patterned. They grow an inch tall (a few centimetres) at most. They have their growth phases during what is fall and winter in North America and Europe. In the spring, they lose their plump form and dry out to a paperlike skin. Underneath this, the new leaf pair for the following year already has been created.

Care: Not quite easy; requires some experience. Location should be sunny, airy, without drafts. During the rest period in the summer, keep them mostly dry. Now and then, mist them in the evening. Keep the plants outside only in pots that are lowered into the ground with a rain protection. In the winter, water regularly and carefully. Never fertilize with nitrogen, otherwise the plants burst. Repot into a meager soil (peat, pebble, and loam, in a ratio of 1:1:1)

Conophytum pearsonii.

Conophytum bilobum.

Conophytum acutum.

Recommended *Conophytum* Species		
Species	**Blossom Color**	**Diam. of the Blossom**
C. bilobum	Yellow	1¼ inch (30 mm)
C. calculus	Deep yellow	½ inch (12 mm)
C. elishae	Golden yellow	¾ inch (20 mm)
C. ficiforme	White to pink	1 inch (25 mm)
C. frutescens	Deep orange to copper yellow	1 inch (25 mm)
C. globosum	Pale pink	½ inch (12 mm)
C. incurvum	Yellow	⅝ to 1¼ inches (15–30 mm)
C. marginatum	Pink	⅝ inch (15 mm)
C. meyerae	Yellow	
C. minutum	Pink-violet	½ to ⅝ inch (12–15 mm)
C. mundum	Whitish to cream	
C. muscosipapillatum	Golden yellow	1¼ to 1½ inches (30–40 mm)
C. notabile	Copper	
C. pearsonii	Violet pink	⅝ to ⅞ inch (16–22 mm)
C. pellucidum	White	⅓ to ⅜ inch (8–10 mm)
C. ruschii	Mauve–pink	
C. truncatum	Light straw	
C. wettsteinii	Violet-purple	¾ to 1¼ inch (20–30 mm)

only when the plant grows beyond the pot, and do not water then for several days. *Conophytum* are susceptible to mealy bugs and to red spider mites; and also to decay because of poor soil drainage.

Cotyledon

Cotyledon orbiculata.

General notes: *Cotyledon* belongs to the Crassulaceae and includes shrublike plants and stem- and leaf-succulent species from South Africa. The leaves are stiff or soft. The inflorescences have long stems; the flowers are bell-shaped.

Care: Easy. The leaf succulent species do well indoors. Location: sunny, but protected from the full sun; warm, with moderate ground moisture. Keep as dry as possible during the plant's rest period. Temperature: never below 50°F (10°C). Soil: sandy, loamy, and rich with nutrient salts.

Species: *C. ladismithiensis:* small, with reddish blossoms. *C. orbiculata* grows upright; leaves thick, egg-shaped with a silvery wax and bordered in red; red blossoms. *C. paniculata* has red blossoms with soft, fleshy sprouts; *C. reticulata* has greenish yellow ones. *C. undulata* has fleshy, white-ringed, wavy-edged leaves and orange-yellow blossoms. *C. wallichii* is poisonous.

Crassula

Crassula falcata.

Crassula socialis.

General notes: The genus *Crassula* gave the family Crassulaceae its name. *Crassula* ranges from annual plants, to water and swamp plants, to treelike plants, to plants that are perennials and highly succulent. They come from South Africa. With their thick, fleshy, hairy, or ringed leaves, they are among the beauties of any collection. The blossoms are very small, and stand together in umbels. They are vividly colored, and they often have a scent.

Care: Very easy; location, sunny and warm. Give sufficient water during the growth period from summer to fall; at other times, water cautiously and from below. Give them light in the winter rest period, otherwise the plants degenerate. Soil: nutritious, loamy, and sandy. Propagate by seed or by leaf and head cuttings.

Species: *C. alstonii:* globular leaf rosettes; blossoms yellow-green.

C. arborescens: in pot cultivation grows up to 3 feet tall (1 m); thick-stemmed, branched, gray-green-ringed, red-dotted leaves with a red edge.

C. barbata: leaf edges hairy; blossoms small, white.

C. columnaris: mussel-shaped leaves that are densely arranged like roof tiles.

C. deceptrix is wax-ringed.

C. falcata: very often sold commercially, but mostly as hybrids, e.g., 'Morgan's Beauty.' Thick, sickle-shaped, gray leaves, and nice-smelling, pink blossoms on umbels.

C. lycopodioides has small, scaly, overlapping leaves on slender, upright, branched stems like club moss.

C. multicava has heart-shaped leaves, light pink blossoms, and little shoot plants in the axils of the inflorescences.

C. rupestris turns bright red in the full sun.

C. ovata (jade plant): numerous white blossoms; more rarely pale pink.

C. sarcocaulis: winter-hardy, lancet-shaped leaves, white or pink blossoms.

C. socialis: dainty; forms a mat. Blossoms white, in cymes. Suitable for hanging pots.

Cotyledon orbiculata grows in its native habitat as a shrub up to 5 feet (1.5 m) tall. The white-grey, wax-ringed, smooth-walled leaves have red-brown borders in some varieties.

The wild form of Crassula falcata shows why this species was chosen for cultivation. The vivid pink to scarlet-red little blossoms stand close together in an abundantly branched cyme.

Crassula socialis originates in Southeast Capeland (South Africa), where it creates dense cushions. The leaves, which grow in pairs, folded like a canoe, are up to ¼ inch (5 mm) long; they curl up at the edges like paper.

EXTRA TIP: *Cotyledon wallichii* **contains a strong poison. People with children or pets should not cultivate this species.**

Delosperma

Dioscorea elephantipes
Elephant's Foot

Dudleya

It is best to grow Delosperma cooperi in the summer in a stone garden. As a low-lying, ramified, half-shrub, the plant produces numerous 1½- to 2-inch-wide (4 to 5 cm) purple-red blossom.

Dioscorea elephantipes (syn. Testudinaria elephantipes), the elephant's foot, reveals at a glance how it got its name. The bark of the half-globular caudex is divided into angular tubercles that look like the toes of an elephant's foot.

Dudleya pulverulenta resembles an Echeveria. The many-leaved rosettes grow up to 20 inches (50 cm) in diameter. The leaves have a dense white waxy coating.

Delosperma cooperi.

Dioscorea elephantipes.

Dudleya pulverulenta.

General notes: These plants of the Aizoaceae family grow out of bulbous roots. The prostrate or spreading, more or less ascending, creeping, densely branched bushy or rosette plants carry many white, yellow, or red blossoms from summer to fall. The leaves are round or angular, often covered with light papillae.
Care: Undemanding. Locate in bright sun (during summer outside); do not water too much. During the cold times of year, not below 41°F (5°C) because the plants are susceptible to frost. Provide proper drainage.
Species: *D. cooperi*: prostrate stems, abundantly ramified. The leaves are soft, fleshy, and almost round, with papillae that are arranged in longitudinal rows.
D. echinata (syn. *Trichodiadema echinatum*) is one of the most beautiful species. The leaves are densely covered with white papillae; the blossoms are whitish yellow. Other species: *D. lehmannii*; *D. tradescantoides*.

General notes: This indoor plant grows up to 20 feet (6 m) tall. *Dioscorea* is, according to recent classification, synonymous with *Testudinaria*; it belongs to the monocot yam family (Dioscoreaceae). Out of a bulbous root (caudex) that juts out of the soil surface, branches with large, heart-shaped leaves grow in the winter. Later on, when the globular caudex becomes larger, corklike, polygonal tubercles grow on its bark. The very small, greenish yellow blossoms come out in clusters. In the spring, the shoots die.
Care: Easy. Location: sunny to half-shade. In the summer at the stage when the plants have leaves, keep them moderately humid, otherwise mist only from time to time.
Species: *D. macrostachya* has a caudex that is very similar to the one described above. It originates in Mexico and is cultivated in the United States and in Puerto Rico for pharmaceutical purposes.

General notes: The mostly white-ringed leaves of these Crassulaceae from the southwest of the United States and Mexico sit, partially encircling the stem, in spiral rosettes. Some species create mats. The inflorescences spring out of the leaf axils. The blossoms, arranged in panicles, are white, yellow, orange, or red.
Care: Location should be very sunny. In the summer, only those without rings can be kept outside. Water regularly, but not on leaves that have white powder, because otherwise the floury coating disappears. Winter rest period: light, above 59°F (15°C), and as dry as possible. Propagate by leaf cuttings, rosettes, and seed.
Species: *D. brittonii*, with its pale-yellow blossoms, is especially pretty. *D. densiflora*: white blossoms. *D. farinosa*: inflorescences up to 14 inches (35 cm) tall. *D. pulverulenta*: dense, goblet-shaped rosettes on a thick stem; inflorescences, with reddish-yellow blossoms, up to 32 inches tall (80 cm).

Echeveria

Echeveria derenbergii.

⬙ ○ 🌡 🗑 🐌

General notes: *Echeveria* are Crassulaceae from Texas, Central America, and northwestern South America. Their decorative leaves are usually arranged in spiral rosettes. Besides species with white-ringed, reddish blue-green, or dark purplered bare leaves, there are also leaves with fine hair, which look and feel like velvet. The blossoms, yellow to red, are especially pretty and numerous in a lot of hybrids.

Care: In general, without problems. They need a sunny, airy spot; in the summer, outside. Sandy, humous soil that is low in nitrogen and careful watering (never into the rosettes or rot threatens) are recommended. Winter rest period in a light, not too warm spot, below 50°F (10°C), and the plants have to be kept rather dry. Only hairy species can tolerate over 50°F (10°C). Propagate by leaf cuttings, and by head cuttings.

Species: *E. agavoides* looks like a reddish mini-agave,

Echeveria pulvinata.

with dark yellow blossoms on top.

E. derenbergii forms a dense mat made of globular to cylindrical rosettes. Its blossoms are reddish yellow; inside they are yellow. The hybrid *E. derenbergii* var. *major* is the most popular.

E. elegans, without a stem, has long runners, alabaster-colored, ringed leaves, and yellow blossoms with pink on top.

E. gibbiflora has several varieties: var. *metallica* has bronze-colored leaves; var. *crispata* has wavy leaf edges.

E. leucotricha, one of the most beautiful white species, has red blossoms.

E. multicaulis remains small and has reddened leaf edges and reddish blossoms that are yellow inside.

E. pilosa and the half-shrublike *E. pulvinata* belong to the hairy species.

E. secunda is often used for the planting of a carpet garden. It has pale-blue-ringed leaves (especially in var. *glauca*), 12-inch-long (30 cm) inflorescences, and very red blossoms.

E. setosa has red-yellow blossoms and leaves with white bristles.

Echeveria derenbergii is a widespread species. The globular rosettes, created by numerous, wide spatulalike, floury-ringed, red-sprayed leaves, are especially valued for their pretty 3- to 4-inch (8 to 10 cm) tall inflorescences with little reddish yellow blossoms.

Echeveria pulvinata, sometimes called the plush plant, has soft, white-haired, egg-shaped, splayed-out leaves about ³/₈-inch thick (1 cm). Its red or yellow-red blossoms grow on horizontally branched inflorescences.

EXTRA TIP: Place ringed and hairy *Echeveria* in locations that are as sunny and airy as possible, so that they remain compact and the leaf surface does not turn green.

Euphorbia

General notes: Of the 2,000 plants in the spurge family (Euphorbiaceae), about 200 are succulents. The succulents do not have many shapes. When they are not blooming, certain species resemble cacti so much that they are also called the cacti of the Old World, since they almost exclusively live in Africa, the Arabian peninsula, and India. The collector can choose among cushion-forming, shrublike, treelike, columnar and globe shapes, and among species with or without spines. The blossoms are strange (see p. 24 and 25).

Care: *Euphorbia* require warm, heated, and sunny locations, never below 54°F (12°C). Water too little, rather than too much, especially in the winter. The soil should be sandy, with humus and loam. Propagate with cuttings (let them bleed out first) or seed (all globe shapes).

Species: *E. canariensis* grows with one shoot or is basally branched.

E. candelabrum has greenish-white striped young sprouts.

E. caput-medusae (Medusa's head) grows rosettes out of long, spreading, snake-shaped branches.

E. grandicornis has coarse spines.

E. horrida (African milk-barrel) has mostly low, ribbed stems that do not have many branches.

E. milii (crown-of-thorns) has many very popular varieties with red, yellow, or cream-colored blossoms.

E. obesa is melon-shaped.

Euphorbia canariensis.

Euphorbia atropurpurea.

Euphorbia milii var. longifolia.

Euphorbia mammillaris.

Euphorbia obesa.

Faucaria

Tiger-jaws

Faucaria tigrina.

General notes: These short-stemmed, mat-forming, lumpy members of the carpetweed family (Aizoaceae) have a common characteristic feature: the dentate leaf edges. On young leaves, the teeth interlock, therefore the name "tiger jaws." The rosettelike leaves, which stand opposite each other like crosses, have white patterns and stand densely together. The yellow blossoms last several days.
Care: The plants are suited for indoor cultivation and are without problems. Choose a very light, airy location; water abundantly during summer, in the winter not at all, otherwise they do not bloom. Soil: earth and sand mixture.
Species: *F. tigrina*, the best known species, is almost exclusively found these days as a cross with other species. It has gray-green leaves with white rows of dots and strong, backwards-bent teeth, which taper off to a point. *F. felina*, *F. lupina*, *F. subindurata*, and *F. tuberculosa* are similar.

Fenestraria

Fenestraria aurantiaca.

General notes: The club-shaped window leaves of these Aizoaceae have a layer without any chlorophyll, through which light falls onto the cellular layers below, which do contain chlorophyll. In their native habitats in southern Africa, only the upper leaf parts protrude from the ground. In cultivation, the leaves have to jut out of the soil, otherwise they rot. The plant makes white or yellow blossoms in the late summer.
Care: Not very easy to cultivate. Locate in very light, bright sun; during the growth period, water only enough to keep the leaves from shrinking. Winter rest period: completely dry at above 59°F (15°C). Soil: sand and loam, as well as perlite, pumice, or similar things. Propagate by seed or leaf cuttings. Repotting is not liked by the plant.
Species: *F. aurantiaca*, with long-stemmed, golden-yellow blossoms. *F. aurantiaca* var. *rhopalophylla*, with shorter, clublike leaves and white blossoms. Crosses of both species are cultivated.

Frithia pulchra

Frithia pulchra.

General notes: This South African member of the Aizoaceae family resembles *Fenestraria*, but is smaller. The two species are differentiated by the fact that the leaves of *Frithia* are rough on top and alternate; in *Fenestraria* they are smooth and opposite each other in pairs. Also, the gray-green, upright-standing, cylindrical leaves of *Frithia*, which are flattened at the ends, are translucent at the upper ends. The blossoms are carmine-red with a white center, more rarely completely white, and last very long.
Care: Requires some experience. Location: very light and warm, at best under glass. Since the plants have their growth period during the winter, they have to be watered then, but only very carefully. In the summer, keep them dry. The flowering time is from June to August.
Species: The only species is *F. pulchra*.

Faucaria tigrina, tiger-jaws, can be placed as an individual plant, because older plants form clumps, and thus fill a somewhat larger pot.

The golden-yellow blossoms of Fenestraria aurantiaca var. rhopalophylla are many times larger than the small bodies, which are thickened and clublike towards the top. On close examination, the windows at the flat leaf ends can be seen.

In contrast to Fenestraria, the Frithia pulchra has coarse window surfaces. Older plants grow like mats.

Gasteria

Gibbaeum

Gasteria hybrid.

There are about 70 Gasteria species, of which many, like the plant pictured here, are bastards or hybrids and often cannot be named exactly. This Gasteria distinguishes itself by its white-speckled leaves.

In Gibbaeum pilosulum, the new leaf pair arches out, as is typical for this genus, with two uneven-sized halves between the still fleshy old pair of leaves. Dried out, dying, and growing leaves and blossoms can be seen at the same time.

General notes: These succulent members of the lily family (Liliaceae), from South Africa and Namibia, at first form fan-shaped leaves in two rows; later, spiral-shaped rosettes, and inflorescences in clusters or in panicles.

Care: Very easy. Needs a sunny or shady spot. Water regularly in the summer; in the winter, keep rather dry and above 50°F (10°C). The soil should have humus, and a lot of pumice, perlite, or similar substances. Propagation is by shoot or leaf cuttings and seed.

Species: *G. armstrongii* has short, rounded leaves.

G. liliputana is very small and very attractive; leaves are white-speckled.

G. maculata has striking leaf speckles.

G. pulchra has shiny green leaves with white, irregular horizontal bands.

G. verrucosa (warty aloe; wart gasteria) is the best-known white, warty species.

× *Gastrolea* are crossings with aloes, very varied in their appearance.

Gibbaeum pilosum.

General notes: These cushion-forming members of the carpetweed family (Aizoaceae) from the Cape region of South Africa include species with very varied forms. The sprouts have one or two thick, fleshy egg- to globe-shaped, pale-green to whitish leaf pairs. In some species, the leaf pairs grow together except for a small cleft; they are spread apart in other species. Often the leaves of a pair are of unequal size. The resulting crooked look is characteristic. The white or pink-violet blossoms appear at the beginning of the winter growth period.

Care: Not very easy. Location: very light, especially for white species. During the rest period in the summer, keep absolutely dry; water carefully only when the first signs of the new growth are visible. After the flowering time, slowly cease to water. If necessary, provide an additional light source in winter; always keep above 59°F (15°C).

Species: *G. album*, with unequal-sized, white feltlike leaves, which grow together into a "crooked egg" shape. The cleft is at first hardly visible, but splits open more later on. White blossoms. Very sensitive, therefore difficult to keep.

Glottiphyllum

Tongueleaf

G. *dispar*, with a velvety leaf surface; violet-red blossoms at the beginning of the winter.

G. *heathii* forms almost globular, ¾- to 1-inch tall (2–3 cm) gray to whitish green bodies; the leaf surface is smooth. The blossoms are ¾ to 1 inch in size (2–3 cm) and are cream-colored to pale pink.

G. *pilosulum* has upside-down egg-shaped, light green, matte plant bodies with fine hair. The cleft between the grown-together leaves is notched and lateral. Violet-red blossoms at the end of December or beginning of January.

G. *schwantesii* has strongly spread, somewhat crooked-keeled, dark to brownish green, velvetlike, hairy leaves of unequal length and large, pure-white blossoms.

G. *velutinum* grows like a mat; the branches are recumbent and are enveloped by dried-out leaves. The leaves only grow together at the base. They are variously shaped and keeled on the back side. The carmine-pink blossoms appear in the fall.

Glottiphyllum linguiforme.

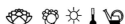

General notes: These fast-growing, abundantly flowering Aizoaceae originate in South Africa. The forklike little stems carry thick-fleshed, tongue-shaped leaves; in some species, they are transparently dotted. In full sun, the leaves turn red. The large blossoms are yellow and dandelionlike.

Care: Without difficulties; suitable for beginners. Location: very sunny; in the summer, can be outside, protected from the rain—but never directly in the ground (they degenerate otherwise). Fertilize the loamy soil only a little; water extremely sparsely. Plant in small pots. Propagate by cuttings; seed may be hybridized.

Species: G. *davisii*: very small. G. *depressum*: low-lying. G. *grandiflorum*: large blossoms. G. *jacobsenianum*: nice-smelling blossoms. G. *linguiforme*: very well known, rarely pure species. G. *nelii*: forms clusters. G. *oligocarpum*: has whitish to olive leaves, but only with a lot of sun. G. *parvifolium*: blossoms that are 3 inches (8 cm) in size.

Graptopetalum

Graptopetalum bellum.

General notes: These mat-forming rosette shrubs from Mexico and the southern USA, related to *Echeveria* and *Pachyphytum* (all are Crassulaceae), have upright or low-lying stems with thick-fleshed leaves. The star-shaped blossoms stand in loose cymes, and the corollas are dark-speckled.

Care: Easy. Location: airy, light, sunny, with protection from the full sun. Water moderately, during the flowering time more; in the winter, very rarely. In winter, keep below 59°F (15°C), or they won't bloom.

Species: G. *amethystinum*: up to 16 inches long (40 cm), with bluish-red leaves and white blossoms. G. *bellum* (syn. *Tacitus bellus*) makes compact, recumbent rosettes of gray-green and opulent carmine-red blossoms. G. *filiferum*: dainty, makes cushions. The speckled corolla petals are typical. G. *paraguayense* (mother-of-pearl plant) has leaf colors that change from plant to plant.

Glottiphyllum blossoms appear from August to February. The tongue-shaped leaves are especially prominent on Glottiphyllum linguiforme, the most famous species of the genus.

Graptopetalum bellum, also known as Tacitus bellus (quiet beauty), has earned its name rightfully. The plant is beautiful when it is not blooming and is even more so when it is in bloom. The blue-violet ringed leaves are then topped by carmine, striped, dotted blossoms.

Haworthia

Haworthia attenuata is recognizable by the white tubercles that densely cover the dark-green leaves.

Haworthia cymbiformis blooms relatively inconspicuously. It creates numerous stemless rosettes that grow together into dense cushions. The slightly transparent leaves turn pale carmine red in intense sunlight.

The light-green rosettes of Haworthia cuspidata look like pieces of jewelry made by the hands of a master. Here, the variety var. willmoriensis.

Haworthia truncata is one of the window-forming species of this genus. The leaves are arranged like a fan, in two rows.

General notes: These lily plants (Liliaceae) from South Africa have been in cultivation for a long time. Most of the species, which remain small and grow in matlike groups, are stemless rosette plants with fleshy leaves that have pearlike tubercles. The leaf edges are often dentate, or ciliate, and the leaf ends are pointy or blunt. The blossoms are small, whitish, and inconspicuous.

Care: Not very difficult. Although *Haworthia* tolerate half-shade, they prefer locations where it is bright. The window-leaf plants even want to be in the sun. Although the window-leaf plants grow deep in their native habitat, they have to be planted at a "normal" depth in cultivation; they are also more sensitive to cold. All *Haworthia* want to be kept cool during the winter, but they are not winter-hardy. *Haworthia* should be repotted regularly, because every year they thrust off a part of their roots, which then rot in the pot. Many species grow in the summer, but some also grow in the winter. During the time of their growth, water regularly. During the rest period, they should never dry out completely. Since the genus tends to create hybrids, one is better off to propagate with little rosettes or cuttings. In pure sand, these grow roots in a short period of time.

Species: *H. attenuata* forms groups of small rosettes out of longish, pointy leaves with tubercles, which flow together in horizontal bands.

Haworthia attenuata.

Haworthia cymbiformis.

Haworthia cuspidata.

Haworthia truncata.

Haworthia coarctata.

Haworthia herbacea.

Haworthia arachnoidea.

Haworthia baccata.

Haworthia retusa.

In the variety var. *clariperla*, the leaves are completely covered with small white tubercles.

H. bolusii creates especially beautiful rosettes out of pale green leaves that are covered with white bristle hair at the edges. The rosettes close up when it is very dry and open up again when it is humid.

H. fasciata has large white tubercles on the underside of coarse green leaves.

H. margaritifera has larger coarse, fleshy leaves with large round white tubercles. It is very variable.

H. maughanii has round rosette leaves. The ends look as if they had been cut off, and the tops are windowed. A magnificent species.

H. reinwardtii has longer stems and olive-green leaves spirally arranged around the stem. The leaves are densely covered with white tubercles, which turn red in the sunlight. Several varieties.

H. setata has rosettes of longish leaves with transparent bristles at the ends.

H. truncata is one of the species with window leaves. The leaves look as if they have been sharply cut off at the ends, and they are arranged like a fan, not like a rosette. The surface is warty, and the blunt end is transparent.

H. venosa has a net of dark leaf nerves, which are easily visible through the transparent upper skin of the leaf. Other interesting species are: *H. guttata*, *H. arachnoidea*, *H. retusa* var. *acuminata*, and *H. cuspidata*.

Haworthia coarctata is also known by the name Haworthia chalwinii.

Haworthia herbacea stands out because of its dentate leaves and its fresh green color.

Haworthia arachnoidea looks as if it has been enveloped by cobwebs. Its species name hints at that fact.

Haworthia baccata has pearllike little tubercles on the leaves, a decoration typical of many Haworthia species.

In Haworthia retusa, the upper half of the leaf bends strongly backwards and functions as a window. In its native habitat, Haworthia retusa is buried in the ground up to the leaf part with the window. The photo shows the variety var. acuminata.

EXTRA TIP: *Haworthia* are pieces of jewelry in green. A bowl about 12 inches (30 cm) in diameter is big enough for a collection of many species. Make sure that the water can drain well, however.

Hoodia

Huernia

The plate-shaped blossoms of Hoodia gordonii have very small lobe tips. The edges are bent somewhat outwards. The flesh-colored to brownish surface is lined by lighter grooves.

The 5 to 7 slender, lightly and finely dentated sprouts of Huernia schneideriana grow up to 8 inches tall (20 cm). The 1-inch (3 cm) blossoms appear on young shoots.

Huernia macrocarpa is an especially unusual species; there is also a small-blossomed variety, var. arabica, with slender, four-sided, fresh green shoots.

Hoodia gordonii.

☀ 🌡 🕭 ⌖ 🪴

Huernia schneideriana.

○ 🌡 ⊍ ⌖ 🪴

Huernia macrocarpa.

General notes: These members of the Asclepiadaceae, whose sprouts are strongly branched at the base and grow up to 39 inches tall (1 m), originate in the semi-deserts of southern Africa. Tubercles that taper off to points sit on many ribs. The mostly reddish, pointed blossoms are circular.

Care: Difficult. A very warm location in the bright sun is optimal; never cooler than 59°F (15°C). Water rather less than too much; in the winter not at all. Seedlings are very susceptible to mycosis. One should graft them and the very root-sensitive species onto *Ceropegia woodii*. Propagation, by cuttings in pure sand, takes up to one year.

Species: *H. bainii*: abundantly branched; blue-green, cylindrical sprouts are spirally covered with tubercles that have spines; blossoms, light orange.

H. currori: branched out, pale gray-green sprouts with many sharp spines; yellowish-pink blossoms.

H. gordonii: key-shaped flesh-colored blossoms.

General notes: The blossoms of the mat-creating *Huernia* appear on young, branched little stems. They are bell-shaped, very diversely colored, dotted or striped, often pointy, with papillae on the surface or with hairs, and they smell like a carcass. The native habitat of these Asclepiadaceae is South Africa, Ethiopia, and Arabia.

Care: Easy. Location: light and sunny; in the summer protect from the full noonday sun. Water only enough to keep the sprouts from shrinking. Soil: sandy, with a small portion of peat, porous. The seeds sprout fast but they are rarely pure species; propagate with cuttings or segmentation.

Species: *H. aspera* has low-lying branches, a wide bell-shaped corolla with triangular tips; reddish blossoms on the outside, purple-brown and dotted on the inside. Blooms easily.

H. bicampanulata carries two-colored blossoms consisting of two bell-shaped parts, which are placed on top of each other.

H. concinna: pale-green

sprouts with a reddish shine; blossoms with tips that have red marks.

H. hystrix has a yellow, scented, red-marked corolla.

H. macrocarpa: five-sided, dentate sprouts. Blossoms, greenish yellow on the outside, light yellow with concentric, red-brown horizontal stripes on the inside. Var. *arabica* has dark purple blossoms with little white hairs.

H. occulata: easy care. Blossoms have white tubes and purple-colored tips.

H. pillansii, with its red-marked yellowish blossoms, is one of the most beautiful.

H. primulina: abundant yellow blooms from early summer to the fall.

H. reticulata: yellowish blossom tips with irregular, netlike spots; blossom tube dark red inside.

H. schneideriana: velvetlike blossoms, brownish on the outside; black inside, with a pink border.

H. zebrina (and *H. confusa*): the most beautiful blossoms of the genus; brown tube-rings and yellow, carmine-red striped tips.

Kalanchoe

Kalanchoe beharensis.

Kalanchoe tubiflora.

Kalanchoe daigremontiana.

General notes: The *Kalanchoe* are leaf succulents from the Crassulaceae family. As indoor plants, they are especially easy to take care of and are rewarding. The most beautiful species come from Madagascar; others, from Africa and Asia. Hardly any other succulent genus is as diverse. Herbs, but also dwarflike, low shrubs; little trees 6½ to 10 feet (2 to 3 m) tall; even epiphytes and lianalike hanging plants belong to it. The often very decorative leaves are bare or hairy, smooth or lobed, or even feathered. Often they or the inflorescences carry little shoot plants that have roots. The blossoms stand upright or hang in the inflorescences; they appear in many colors from white or greenish to all shades of red and yellow. The *Kalanchoe* are short-day plants. They only bloom when they have less than 12 hours of light per day. Therefore, they can be brought into bloom throughout the year, guided by the duration of daylight. However, they are generally considered to be winter or prespring bloomers.

Care: The plants need to be where it is bright, sunny, warm, and airy. Only the bare-leaf ones should be outside in the summer. The soil should be sandy and humous, pH 5.5 to 6.5, porous, and low on nitrogen. Water a lot. During winter keep them rather dry and below 50°F (10°C). Often distinct rest periods are missing. Propagate through head or leaf cuttings or shoot leaves. For mass cultivation, use seeds.

Species: *K. beauverdii* has dark, speckled blossoms; it is suitable for hanging pots.

K. blossfeldiana is a horticulturally mass-produced plant. The blossoms are yellow, orange, violet, or red (photo on p. 104).

K. daigremontiana (syn. *Bryophyllum daigremontianum*) has tiny plantlets with roots in the axils of the triangular leaves. The blossoms are gray-violet.

K. manginii is a hanging plant with bright red blossoms (photo on p. 105).

K. marmorata has long, gray-ringed, speckled leaves; cream-white blossoms.

K. pinnata has leaves that are at first dentate; later on, feathered; they develop little shoot plants at their edges.

K. pumila is a hanging plant with floury, white-ringed leaves and many reddish violet blossoms.

K. rhombopilosa is a dainty shrub with silver-gray, wine-red speckled leaves and inconspicuous blossoms.

K. scapigera: gray, waxy leaves and bright red blossoms.

K. tomentosa (pussy ears) is one of the most beautiful *Kalanchoe*. The leaves are covered with a white felt and have fox-red hairs at the upper, dentate edges. They grow in a loose rosette around a densely hairy sprout axil. Rarely blooms.

K. tubiflora has tube-shaped, gray-green, reddish speckled leaves with sprout buds that grow at the mother-plant's roots, but only in high air humidity.

K. uniflora: a pretty, epiphytic hanging plant; its bare thick-fleshed leaves are notched at the edges. The leaves stand on long, hanging sprouts. It has large, bright-red blossoms.

Kalanchoe beharensis (velvet elephant-ear) does not look as attractive in its native habitat as it does as a solitary plant of a plant lover. The triangular, lancet-shaped, densely woolly, hairy leaves, which resemble elephant ears, grow up to 12 inches long (30 cm).

The relatively large, bell-shaped, orange blossoms of the robust *Kalanchoe tubiflora* hang on compact inflorescences. The plant develops reddish brown speckled shoot buds.

The upright sprouts of *Kalanchoe daigremontiana* have stemmed, 6- to 8-inch-long (15 to 20 cm) narrow, pointy leaves. The shoot buds grow on the notched leaf edges.

Kalanchoe hybrids

Kalanchoe species with bell-shaped blossoms are popular with professional gardeners. They are taken care of just like all other Kalanchoe species and varieties.

Kalanchoe fedtschenkoi cv. 'Variegata' has, in contrast to the wild form, whitish yellow variegated leaves.

The many little blossoms of Kalanchoe blossfeldiana stand in large numbers in umbels on long stems above the leaves. They last a long time, and in the course of months, new buds continue to open.

Golden-blooming hybrids of Kalanchoe blossfeldiana. The original species of all blossfeldiana hybrids blooms in minium red, from which yellow, orange, pink, red, and violet shades were cultivated.

Kalanchoe flammea is easily grown from seeds. If planted out early enough, it will bloom in the first year. The specimens sold commercially are usually hybrids like Kalanchoe × kewensis.

General notes: Kalanchoe hybrids are so popular that every year millions of them are sold. The favorite one of the growers has been *Kalanchoe blossfeldiana*. There are also varieties of *K. manginii* and other species. The play of colors of *K. blossfeldiana* ranges today from cream to yellow, orange, pink, red, and violet. There are red and yellow-red blooming varieties of *K. manginii*.

Care: See *Kalanchoe* species.

Cultivars: Most of the *Kalanchoe* hybrids go back to *K. blossfeldiana*. The first trade hybrids, 'Alfred Gräser', 'Tom Thumb', 'Vulcan', and 'Gelber Liebling', are still cultivated today. The newer generations in cultivation have larger blossoms, stronger and newer colors, and less root sensitivity. These improvements were achieved by crossing other *Kalanchoe* species.

Kalanchoe with bell-shaped blossoms.

Kalanchoe fedtschenkoi.

Kalanchoe blossfeldiana.

Kalanchoe blossfeldiana hybrid.

Kalanchoe flammea.

Kalanchoe blossfeldiana hybrid.

The many hybrid Kalanchoe blossfeldiana produced, in addition to the fire-red blossoms, many new shades from yellow to dark violet-red. In addition, the growth of the plants is more compact than in the wild form.

Kalanchoe manginii is one of the very small species. The oval sparlike, up to 1-inch-long (3 cm) long leaves have fine hairs in the beginning. The bell-shaped blossoms hang at the ends of blossom branches that are up to 12 inches long (30 cm).

Kalanchoe manginii.

EXTRA-TIP: So that *Kalanchoe* bloom throughout the whole year, one can guide the time of flowering artificially. For that, the plants must remain at least 5 to 6 weeks, for less than 12 hours per day, in very bright light; then in absolute dark; after another 4–5 weeks, they will bloom. After the short days, long days should be offered, i.e., the plants are artificially illuminated for more than 12 hours (up to 19 hours) daily. That holds true especially for plants from which one takes cuttings.

Lithops

Living Stones

Lithops koelermannii belongs to the group of the yellow-blooming living stones and is distinguished especially by its rust-brown body.

In Lithops divergens, individual or multiple plant bodies appear with deeply gaping clefts. The windows are large, transparent, and light gray-green or finely furrowed.

A collection of various Lithops species in the nonflowering stage. The similarity to the pebbles that surround it is stunning. Perfect camouflage!

Large, coffee- to rust-brown, or olive-green bodies are the hallmark of Lithops lesliei, which is, by the way a very variable species.

Lithops karasmontana has a pitlike furrowed top surface. The furrows are bordered in brownish ochre, which has a striking effect against the bluish-yellow-gray of the body.

EXTRA-TIP: *L. optica f. rubra,* the most popular rarity, has purple-red plant bodies with windows that clearly stand out.

○ 🌡 🧊 🗑

General notes: In their native habitat, the rock-strewn deserts of South Africa and Namibia, one finds these members of the carpetweed family (Aizoaceae) only when they bloom. Otherwise, they look just like stones. The inverted-cone-shaped body of the plant consists of thick, fleshy leaves, which grow together except for a small cleft. Each year, two leaves are produced, at right angles to the old pair of leaves. The side parts contain chlorophyll. The flat ends of the leaves are often transparent ("windowed") and patterned. The growth period ends when the white or yellow blossoms come out of the cleft.

Care: Easy to cultivate. Location: airy and sunny. Water only during the time of growth, sparsely. When watered too much, the bodies burst. From September on, keep them completely dry. Winter rest period: light, at 59°F (15°C). The plants keep their typical form only in meager, sandy soil, containing very little loam and even less humus. Propagate by seed; hardly ever through cuttings.

Species: *Yellow-blooming: L. aucampiae, L. bromfieldii, L. comptonii, L. divergens, L. helmutii, L. herrei, L. lesliei, L. localis, L. otzeniana, L. turbiniformis.* **White-blooming:** *L. bella, L. fulleri, L. karasmontana, L. lesliei var. lesliei f. albiflora, f. albinica, L. marmorata, L. optica f. rubra, L. salicola, L. villetii.*

Lithops koelermannii.

Lithops divergens.

Various Lithops species.

Lithops lesliei.

Lithops karasmontana.

Monadenium

Monadenium guentheri.

○ ◗ 🗄 ☠

General notes: These stem succulent members of the Euphorbiaceae from tropical Africa are treelike or succulent shrubs with long, cylindrical, warty-edged stems; also root succulents with nonsucculent above-ground plant parts. All plants produce a poisonous sap (latex) and have unusual blossoms.
Care: Most species are easy to cultivate. Location: sunny and warm, as with *Euphorbia:* do not water too much. Use porous soil that is very low on calcium sulfate. Propagate by cuttings.
Species: *M. coccineum* grows unbranched sprouts with fleshy, dentate leaves and red inflorescences. *M. ellenbeckii* has small yellow-green high leaves, which soon fall off, on long, grooved stems. *M. guentheri* has long, warty branches, growing in an arch upwards, with fleshy leaves that are wavy at the edge. The high leaves are greenish white and marbled in purple. *M. lugardae* grows thick sprouts from a bulbous root; leaves, pointy and hairy; with very small thorns.

Oophytum

Oophytum oviforme.

○ ◗ 🗄

General notes: These plants from the carpetweed family (Aizoaceae) form two pairs of leaves during each vegetative period. The leaves grow to globular or egg-shaped bodies that are enveloped by the paperlike remainders of the leaves from the year before. The red or white blossoms appear individually. In their native South Africa, the plants grow clumped or like a mat, and can grow on ground that contains salt. Cultivation is not quite easy; follow the cultivation notes given for *Conophytum.*
Care: During the vegetative period in the winter, place them where it is sunny, light, and warm; water only moderately. During the rest period in the summer, keep them absolutely dry. Water again only when new leaf rudiments are clearly showing.
Species: *O. nanum:* an almost globular body and white blossoms with red tips.
 O. oviforme: an egg-shaped body and white, red-pointed blossoms up to ¾-inch (2 cm) in diameter.

Ophthalmophyllum

Eye-Leaves

Ophthalmophyllum praesectum.

☀ ◗ 🥛 🗄

General notes: These members of the Aizoaceae family from south and southwest Africa resemble *Lithops.* The dwarf plants usually have only one soft-fleshed, stemless shoot. The body is a single, cylindrical or slightly club-shaped pair of leaves, divided by a notch or cleft. The leaf ends are mostly transparent (windowed). Depending on the species, the leaves are green, reddish or purple-red, smooth or fine-haired. The blossoms are white, pink, or light carmine red.
Care: Requires some experience. Location: in bright sun and warmth. Growth begins in the fall; then one must water very sparsely. All species are especially sensitive to standing water; therefore, keep them in porous, sandy soil.
Species: *O. dinteri:* reddish green with transparent windows and violet-red blossoms. *O. friedrichiae:* green to copper-red body, windows transparent, as clear as water; white blossoms.
O. villetii: body hairy on top; arched window; pale pink striped blossoms.

Monadenium guentheri has warty, cylindrical, fleshy sprouts and inflorescences with short stems that grow at the sprout ends. The outer leaves are greenish white and purple-marbled.

Oophytum oviforme grows like a large mat, created by numerous globular to egg-shaped, olive-green to bright red bodies that stand close together. The large white blossoms are purple-red at the tips.

Ophthalmophyllum praesectum blooms reddish violet. The cylindrical plant bodies are up to 1 inch long (3 cm) and feel almost like velvet.

Oscularia

Pachyphytum

Pachyphytum oviferum belongs in every succulent collection. The rosettes created by the thick-fleshed, inverted-egg-shape, pink-circled leaves attract the eye immediately.

General notes: The sprouts of these flatly spread out, strongly branched, small South African members of the carpetweed family (Aizoaceae) are reddish when they are young; later on woody. The three-angled leaves, which are grown together somewhat at the base, are striped gray-green to blue-green, and dentate; they become red-edged in the sun. The small, short-stemmed, pink to red blossoms appear in the spring or summer, usually in threes.

Care: Very undemanding; well suited for beginners. Location: light and warm. Growth and rest periods are not strictly separated, but water very little in the winter and keep them somewhat cooler. Propagate by seed or cuttings.

Species: *O. caulescens*: reddish branches, blue-gray-ringed leaves, and pink blossoms with an almond scent. *O. deltoides*: light-gray-ringed leaves, whose edges and outer parts are red-toothed; many nice-smelling pink blossoms.

Pachyphytum oviferum.

General notes: These smooth members of the Crassulaceae family, which are related to the *Echeveria*, are native to Mexico. The rosette plants are stemless or form upright, rather thick, short, branched stems. The loosely standing leaves are thick, smooth, roundish, and often covered with a whitish bloom. The large reddish or white blossoms appear on branched inflorescences, which at first nod, then stand upright.

Care: Without problems. Location: like *Echeveria*, light and in bright sun at the window. In the winter, keep them cooler and water very little. Do not water from the top. Propagation is by leaf cuttings.

Species: *P. oviferum* is the most beautiful species. Egg-round thick, whitish-gray-ringed leaves with a touch of red stand at the short, white-ringed sprout axils. The inflorescence has greenish white blossoms. *P. bracteosum*: red blossoms. *P. hookeri*: gray-blue leaves and light-red blossoms.

Pachypodium

Madagascar palm tree

Pachypodium lamerei.

☼ 🌡 🖐 ⌂

General notes: These stem-succulent plants of the Apocynaceae come from South Africa and Madagascar. The tree-shaped species are ones usually under cultivation. They form a water-storing caudex with spirally arranged, thorny tubercles. On the sprout a leaf rosette sits, which falls off during the plant's rest period.

Care: Easy. Location: sunny, light, and warm; especially warm at the ground. They can tolerate dry room air. Water only in the stage in which the plant has leaves; then, rather a lot. Provide proper drainage. The soil should be porous and humous, with quartz sand and perlite. Propagate by seed. They are susceptible to red spider mites.

Species: *P. geayi:* thorny, with silver-gray leaves. *P. lamerei:* conical, much-branched fleshy trunk to 6 feet (2 m) tall; has several varieties, including a cristate form with colorful leaves. *P. baronii* (red blossoms); the variety *P. windsori* will bloom in cultivation.

Pedilanthus

Slipper

Pedilanthus tithymaloides.

◐ 🌡 🗑 🖐 ☠

At the bottom, Pachypodium lamerei looks like a cactus; at the top, like a palm tree. In the 1970s, when the first specimens showed up in the flower trade, it was a real sensation.

Pedilanthus tithymaloides cv. 'Variegatus' is a white-speckled, horticultural cultivar, grown as a decorative shrub.

General notes: This bushy to clustering or branched genus of the Euphorbiaceae family from the southern United States, Central America, and the Caribbean carries very small, often white-green leaves, on woody, succulent sprouts; the leaves fall off at the end of the vegetative time. The roundish little stems have a poisonous latex. The shoe-shaped, diagonal blossom in yellowish green, pink, red, or brown is very striking.

Care: Locate in a sunny place or in half-shade. Water moderately. Absolutely avoid high air humidity at cool temperatures. The soil should be porous and humous, in deep pots. The plants are susceptible to powdery mildew. Propagation is easy with cuttings.

Species: *P. macrocarpus:* branched growth; hairy sprouts and high leaves. *P. smallii:* white-colored. *P. tithymaloides* (syn. *P. carinatus*): many species, with variegated leaves on slightly zigzag-shaped branches, bright-red high leaves.

EXTRA TIP:
Based on experience, we know that *Pachypodium lamerei* blooms from a height of 4 feet (120 cm) on, with magnificent white blossom-stars.

Pelargonium

Pleiospilos

Living-Rock

Pleiospilos bolusii.

Pelargonium carnosum.

To take care of a succulent Pelargonium can be very rewarding. Although the blossoms are, in comparison to the magnificence of more showy geraniums, rather plain, the plant has quite an exotic look, as Pelargonium carnosum demonstrates with its thick stems.

Pleiospilos bolusii, with yellow to orange blossoms, is a typical representative of this highly succulent genus. In its native habitat, the coloration adapts itself to the rock debris around it.

General notes: Many members of this South African succulent species, with their bizarre growth, are completely different in their appearance from the well-known geranium plants. These shrubs from the geranium family (Geraniaceae) have branched, swollen stems with a cork coat or a wax coating. Some species form false thorns from dried-out side leaves, or from woody inflorescences. During the dry period, the leaves are absent. The blossoms are plain.

Care: Somewhat demanding. Location: very bright, sunny, and warm—at least 59°F (15°C). During the growth period in the winter, the feathered leaves appear. At that time, water sparsely. Keep the plant dry in the summer. Use porous, sandy, and humous soil. Propagation by seed; more rarely by cuttings.

Species: *P. carnosum:* thick stems, feathered leaves, and white blossoms. Other species: *P. ceratophyllum, P. cotyledonis, P. crithmifolium, P. echinatum,* and *P. fulgidum.*

General notes: Most of these dwarf members of the Aizoaceae, which grow like a mat, consist only of a gray-green, stemless leaf pair; more rarely of two to four leaves. In form and color, they resemble rocks. The leaves grow together at the base; on the underside, they are distinctly arched and transparently dotted. The bright-yellow day blossoms are very large and come out at the end of the summer.

Care: Easy. Location: sunny, bright. During the growth period only, from May to July, should one water, carefully. During the other months let the plant remain completely dry. Soil: sandy, loamy. The plants must be in deep pots because of their long tap roots. Propagation is easy with seed; also with cuttings.

Species: *P. bolusii:* two leaves that are dark, flattened on the top, and dotted brownish-green. *P. nelii:* half-globular, dark gray-green, densely dotted leaves; blossoms, orange to salmon-pink. *P. nobilis:* short, woody stem and thick, gray-green, speckled leaves.

Plumeria

Frangipani, Temple Tree

Plumeria alba.

☼ 🌡 🥤 🖐 🐛 ☠

General notes: The temple tree is a symbol for immortality in the Buddhist culture. It is among the most beautiful flowering trees of the tropical regions. In temperate countries, it is usually kept as a tub plant. Actually, the frangipani, from the Apocynaceae family, which grow everywhere in tropical regions, originate in Central America and the Caribbean Islands. The trees or bushes, over 13 feet tall (4 m), have a thick, fleshy stem and succulent, deep-green branches, which divide regularly. The spirally standing, long-stemmed, thick, leathery leaves, which fall off during the plant's rest period, have a sap that contains poisonous alkaloids. The leaves grow up to 18 inches (½ m) long, but only 6 inches (15 cm) wide. The large, nice-smelling, multicolored blossoms, which appear in the summer at the ends of the sprouts in cymes, are gorgeous.
Care: Location: in the full sun; in the summer, can be outside. During the vegetative time, water and fertilize

Plumeria rubra.

moderately; let the plant remain dry in the winter. The rest period (when the leaves fall off) is important for the formation of blossom buds. The temperatures must not go below 59°F (15°C) during the cold time of the year. Soil: sand, loam, or clay, and some humus. Susceptible to an attack of red spider mites. Propagate by seed and well-dried cuttings.
Species: *P. acuminata* (syn. *P. acutifolia*) has large, longish leaves, white blossom buds, and white blossoms that are yellow on the in-

side. *P. alba:* a summer-green, round tree up to 13 feet (4 m) tall; 12-inch-long (30 cm) lancet-shaped leaves. Blossoms stand in clusters at the shoot tips; they are white with a yellow eye and they have a pleasant smell. *P. purpurea:* blossoms red outside; inside, yellow and hairy. *P. rubra:* a somewhat smaller tree or shrub. In the fall it has bright-red blossoms with yellow throats. A number of hybrids with many blossom colors are sold commercially.

The white blossoms of Plumeria alba grow in large panicles at the ends of the branches. The leaves of this species are rather small in comparison to those of the other representatives of this genus.

On Plumeria rubra one can see how big the leaves are. Even the 1½- to 1-inch-long (3 to 4 cm) blossoms seem small in comparison to them.

EXTRA TIP: Did you know that the perfume "Frangipani," which was created by the Italian Frangipani in the 12th century, did not contain any aromatic substances from *Plumeria*, but a mix of different essential oils? *Plumeria* was only discovered 400 years later; perhaps it was called "Frangipani," because it smelled like the famous perfume.

Portulacaria afra

Elephant Bush

Portulacaria afra (elephant bush) has thick, shiny green leaves that look as if they were greased.

When planted in a low bowl and kept very small, Portulacaria afra easily develops into a bonsailike, bizarre little tree. The tree-shaped growth and the branches, which stick out almost horizontally, reinforce this impression.

Portulacaria afra.

Portulacaria afra as a miniature tree.

General notes: The only species, *Portulacaria afra*, is a very popular indoor plant, native to South Africa. A superstition is attached to it: As long as it grows and prospers, the finances of its owner will be in order. How nice that this plant lives extraordinarily long and is extremely easy to take care of! The elephant bush grows shrublike or tree-shaped. On the sparlike, branched sprouts, which have smooth, gray-brown bark, are leaves that are small, fleshy, oval to round, bare, and evergreen or sometimes beige. The blossoms are small, star-shaped and pink, but they rarely appear in cultivation.

Care: The location should be very bright. If there is not enough light, the shoots grow too long and hang over; thus, the plant loses its typical look. During the growth period from spring to late summer, water regularly and fertilize a little bit. During the rest period in the winter, keep the plant only a little moist. The temperature should not go below 59°F (15°C). In order to get a nice, bushy form, cut the shoots back frequently. Propagation is by seed or half-ripe cuttings in the summer.

Species: *P. afra*: horizontally branched, red-brown, knotty, divided branches. Leaves: shiny green, thick-fleshed, with almost heart-shaped leaf tips. *P. afra* var. *foliis variegatis* has cream-colored to yellow leaves that are bordered in pink. The *Portulaca* species, which, like *Portulacaria*, are members of the family Portulacaceae, are succulent shrubs, of which only *P. grandiflora* produces abundantly blooming outdoor summer flowers in white, yellow, red, and violet.

Ruschia

Ruschia dualis.

○ 🌡 🏺 🌿

General notes: These Aizoaceae from South Africa are small and bunched, the branches ramified and up-right or prostrate. The leaves embrace the stem in a long sheath but only a short part grows together; otherwise the leaves are three-angled, pointed, bluish-green, and dark or transparently dot-ted. The day blossoms grow individually or in multiples. Only a few species open at night.

Care: Not difficult. Loca-tion: sunny and airy, under glass; the taller, shrublike species also can be outdoors. Winter rest pe-riod: light, above 50°F (10°C). Water very little. Propagation is by seed or stem cuttings.

Species: *R. dualis*: grows like a mat; small grayish white leaves; violet-pink blossoms. *R. herrei*: grows like a mat; leaves blue-green with large dots; carina and edges translucent. *R. per-foliata*: larger, shrublike; red blossoms. *R. uncinata*: al-most winter-hardy; not very willing to bloom.

Schwantesia

Schwantesia ruedebuschii.

☼ 🌡 🏺 🌿

General notes: This South African genus from the carpetweed family (Aizoaceae) includes only about 10 species. On very short sprout axils, covered by dry leaf-remainders, two to four unequal pairs of gray-green dentate or pointy leaves stand crossways and opposite. They are wider at the upper end and are cari-nated on the underside. On top they are flat and mar-bled. The edges and carina are reddish. The long-stemmed, large blossoms are yellow. *Schwantesia* are not very willing to bloom.

Care: Somewhat demand-ing. Location: very sunny with little air humidity. Wa-ter only a little. During the winter rest period, keep them dry and not below 59°F (15°C). Propagate by seed, cuttings, or segmentation.

Species: *S. herrei* var. *herrei* f. *major* (syn. *S. loeschiana*): smooth, bluish-white leaves.

S. ruedebuschii: 2-inch-long (5 cm), white-marbled, thick, boat-shaped, arched leaves with little teeth.

Ruschia dualis is a stemless representa-tive of a very large and diversified ge-nus. The small leaf-pairs grow together for about one-third of their length.

As may be seen in Schwantesia ruedebuschii, the crosslike positioning of the leaves, in con-nection with their strange form, creates a very bizarre plant.

Sedum

Stone Crop, Orpine

Here are two plants that like each other and have about the same demands: Sedum and Sempervivum. The golden yellow blossoms of the golden carpet, Sedum acre, are especially pretty when placed next to the wine-red Sempervivum varieties.

Sedum sarmentosum forms runnerlike stems, about 12 inches (30 cm) long, which lie on the ground. The light-yellow blossoms grow in loose cymes. Sedum sarmentosum is susceptible to winter moisture. Tip: Keep cuttings, which very easily grow roots, in the cold-frame during winter and use them to re-place possible losses in the spring.

General notes: These leaf-succulent Crassulaceae from the dry areas of Central America are suitable for room and greenhouse culti-vation. For outdoors, use the winter-hardy species. The leaves, which break off very easily when touched, are of-ten vividly colored, espe-cially when exposed to bright sunshine. The small blossoms are combined in magnificent cymes.

Care: Easy. Location: light and in bright sun; water abundantly in summer; in the winter, keep drier. *Sedum* does not do well at tempera-tures below 50°F (10°C). It has a nondistinct rest pe-riod. Propagate by cuttings.

Species: *S. adolphii*: yellow-ish green, reddish-bordered leaves, white blossoms.

S. lydium: a creeper; blooms from June to July.

S. morganianum (donkey's tail): one of the most beauti-ful hanging plants; has pink to purple-red blossoms.

S. pachyphyllum (jelly-beans): has gray-green leaves with red tips, and yellow blossoms.

S. rubrotinctum: has leaves that turn red in the sun.

S. sieboldii: hanging plant with blue-green, red-bordered leaves and pink blossoms; the var. *variegatis* is especially decorative, with its colorful leaves and yel-lowish white speckles.

S. spathulifolium: creeping; mat-forming; blossoms, light yellow. For outdoors.

S. stahlii: dainty, brown-green, hairy; in the sun be-comes bright red; blossoms, yellowish green.

Sedum acre with Sempervivum.

Sedum sarmentosum.

Sedum rubrotinctum 'Aurora.'

Sedum nussbaumerianum.

Sedum rubrotinctum 'Aurora' is a cultivar that grows very compactly. The leaf coloration varies from a touch of greenish pink to salmon pink (see center photo on bottom).

Sedum nussbaumerianum originates in Mexico and has a strong similarity to Sedum adolphii.

Sedum morganianum, the donkey's tail, grows down rather than up. When free-hanging, the plant, made out of thick, fleshy, silver-gray-ringed, longish lancetlike leaves, which otherwise easily break and fall off, is less likely to be damaged.

Sedum morganianum 'Buretti' has shorter leaves, which do not fall off so easily, and it grows altogether stockier. On the bottom row, at left, is a young plant of this pretty variety.

Sedum sieboldii is a species whose succulence is less noticeable.

Sedum morganianum.

Sedum morganianum 'Buretti.'

Sedum morganianum.

Sedum rubrotinctum 'Aurora.'

Sedum sieboldii.

Sempervivum

Houseleek

Sempervivum arach-noideum looks as if it were covered with spider webs. The in-florescence grows 2 to 6 inches (5 to 15 cm) tall. There are numerous varieties, with different de-grees of hairiness; some are even cov-ered with a dense white felt.

Under intense sun-shine, the green rosettes of the house leek (Sempervivum tectorum) turn wine-red. There are also garden species like Atropurpureum, which have dark-purple rosettes.

Sempervivum arachnoideum.

General notes: The 30 species of this genus from the Crassulaceae family are native to the regions around the Mediterranean, and also to the Near East. In tempe-rate zones, they mainly grow outdoors: on walls, roofs, and in stone gardens. As room plants or under glass, they completely degenerate. They form a dense, low mat or cushion, created by rosettes that easily make runners and divide them-selves. They have fleshy green, reddish, or bluish leaves that are mostly ciliate and hairy at the edges; they are arranged spirally and may be inverted-egg-shaped to lancet-shaped. In the summer, the ramified cymes, with star-shaped, small whitish, yellow, pink or purple-red blossoms ap-pear on older plants. After the flowering time, the rose-ttes die, but because of the numerous runner plants, re-placements are already in place. In long dry periods, the outer leaves of the ro-settes dry up and place themselves protectively around the inside of the

Sempervivum tectorum.

plant, which is thus able to survive.

Care: Location: sunny, outdoors for the entire year. Very meager soil; many spe-cies grow on walls, tile roofs, in dry walls, and on boulders. Propagate by seed or segmentation.

Species: *S. arachnoideum:* green leaves with red tips that are overspun by white hair; loose, carmine-pink blossoms.

S. ciliosum: rosettes of gray-green, hairy leaves; yel-lowish blossoms; forms many runners.

S. giuseppii forms flat mats out of many pea-green, small rosettes. The leaves are very hairy and, espe-cially where the shoots come out, dark-speckled. The red blossoms have white borders.

S. grandiflorum: rosettes created by dark-green, often red-tinted, hairy leaves that smell like goats when one crushes them. Yellow blos-soms on long stems; dark-violet speckled at the bot-tom. The plant needs hu-mous but meager soil.

S. montanum: rosettes

A stone garden planted with different Sempervivum species can be extremely attractive. Sempervivum means "eternally alive," and the plants seem to take this literally. They survive the entire year outdoors, practically without tending.

Various Sempervivum species.

globe-shaped; leaves dark green, fleshy, hairy; blossoms wine-red; inflorescences, long. Many hybrids.

S. tectorum (common houseleek, hen-and-chickens) is the best known species. It is in high demand for growing green plants on roofs. This species, which was already very variable, was cross-bred with so many other species that the hybrid can hardly be overlooked anymore. The many commercial varieties are distinguished above all by leaf-shape and color. They have narrow or wide, pointy, or rounded leaves. The leaf colors are green, gray, bright red, or blue-green, with brown or reddish tips. All houseleek species are very attractive and not very susceptible to diseases. The blossoms stand on high inflorescences and are mostly violet-red, but also: yellowish (S. × hayekii); purple (S. × schottii); pink (S. tectorum ssp. alpinum); or red (S. tectorum ssp. calcareum 'Grigg's Surprise'). Two more Sempervivum are known in the trade by the synonym Jo-vibara: J. hirta: rosettes created by hairy, rather pointy leaves that have a touch of red; forms dense mats; the blossoms are yellow. The plant is a bit sensitive to rain. J. sobolifera: rather large rosettes [up to 8 inches in diameter (20 cm)], created by gray-green or olive-green leaves with a touch of red. Pale-yellow blossoms grow in clusters. The trade variety S. 'Commander Hay' is especially popular because of the very large rosettes created by its dark-red leaves. The blossoms are greenish red.

EXTRA TIP: The common houseleek is not only a healing plant. In Germany it formerly was considered by country people as being protection against lightning when it was grown on the roof. Therefore its German name was *Donnerwurz* (thunderleek).

Senecio

with *Kleinia*

Senecio articulatus folia rubra is a charming variety of this highly individual member of the Compositae; although one may hardly believe it, it is closely related to chamomile.

Senecio rowleyanus forms shoots that hang down and resemble strings of pearls; it is an exceptionally attractive hanging plant, blessed with blossoms that once in a while smell faintly of cinnamon.

Senecio articulatus 'Variegatus.'

General notes: The more than 100 stem- or leaf-succulent species of these composite flowers (Compositae), native to the Canary Islands, Africa, Madagascar, India, and Mexico , are extremely varied in growth and shape. The leaves are flat or cylindrical, and often feltlike. They only have the form of the inflorescence in common: Many very small, tube-shaped blossoms sit densely together on a flat or arched blossom receptacle, surrounded by a calyx of sepals. Some species have only isomorphous blossoms with five-part corollas, so-called disk flowers. Other species have in addition blossoms whose corolla tapers off like a ray on one side, so-called ray flowers. The plant may be a creeper, matlike, shrublike, or climbing.

Care: Very undemanding and easy. Location: light, in bright sun, warm. Less sensitive species also may be outside. Fertilize and water in the summer amply; in the winter only a little bit. *Kleinia* species have a short rest period in the summer

Senecio rowleyanus.

and one in the winter. For the winter rest period, keep the plant where it is light, cool, and not below 50°F (10°C). Propagate by segmentation, cuttings, or seed.

Species: *S. articulatus* (syn. *Kleinia articulata*) has ringed, blue-green, short-limbed sprouts that easily fall off; in old age, they have leaves only at the ends. The yellowish blossoms sit like little heads on a slender, umbelliferous peduncle. This popular species grows fast and is easy to propagate because of its sprouts, which fall off. The variety

var. *globosus* forms almost globular, ⅓ to ¾-inch-long (10–20 mm), ⅓- to ½-inch-thick (10–15 mm) limbs.

S. citriformis grows low-lying or creeping with partially upright shoots. It is distinguished by thick, fleshy, globular, pointed, lemonlike leaves that are blue-gray and waxy-ringed. The blossoms are cream-colored to yellowish.

S. crassissimus forms blue-violet branched sprouts with vertically standing leaves that turn their narrow sides towards the light. The blossoms are yellow.

S. herreianus is a popular hanging plant with globular, windowed leaves on long, hanging sprout axils.

S. kleinia (syn. *Kleinia neriifolia*) has white-ringed green sprouts (in the sun they turn red), which branch out in whorls after the flowering time. In the summer, longish leaves grow at the sprout ends.

S. rowleyanus is known by the common name string-of-beads and resembles *S. herreianus*, but is grows more easily and is blessed with blossoms that smell like cinnamon.

S. scaposus forms rosettes of long, cylindrical leaves that are white and feltlike at the beginning, on short stems. The blossoms are yellow. The variety var. *caulescens* has 16-inch-long (40 cm), finger-thick, ramified little branches. In addition, the leaves are flatter.

S. stapeliiformis has angular sprouts that are branched from the base, similar to those of *Stapelia* , hard-scaled little leaves, and scarlet-red blossoms.

Stapelia

Carrion Flower, Starfish Flower

Stapelia variegata.

Stapelia gigantea.

Stapelia gigantea has indeed gigantically large blossom stars [10 to 14 inches (25 to 35 cm) diameter]. The fine, wavy pattern created by horizontal red calluses looks very subdued on them.

Stapelia variegata has a large number of subspecies and is a frequent crossing partner in hybrids. Who would be surprised, in view of its magnificent appearance?

○ ! 🗑 🪴 🌿

General notes: The plants of this genus of South African stem succulents from the milkweed family (Asclepiadaceae) are not very striking: The soft, fleshy, low-lying or upright, bare or hairy sprout axils are angular and dentate and branch out at the base. The leaves shrivel up to small, dry scales. But the plant makes splendid, huge, often hairy, five-tipped, wheel-shaped blossoms, which are colored vividly, mostly brown. Un-

fortunately the blossoms smell like a carcass.

Care: Location: light, sunny, but protected from the full noonday sun. Water only moderately during the growth period in the summer. During the winter rest period, keep the plant below 64°F (18°C) and dry, but do not let the sprouts shrivel. Use flat containers. Soil: sandy, humous, with a lot of pumice or perlite. Species-true propagation can be done only through segmentation. On the whole, strongly hybridized. Can be

attacked by black rot.

Species: *S. erectiflora*: blossoms purple with dense white hair, rolled-back blossom tips.

S. flavirostris: blossoms purple with yellow lines, tips rolled back.

S. gigantea: blossoms light-yellow with red, callous horizontal bands, slightly reddish hair.

S. grandiflora: blossoms greenish-red on the back side, dark purple on top; edges have reddish or white cilia.

S. longipes: blossoms purple-black with a white- or reddish-speckled center; reddish hair.

S. nobilis: blossoms red; on the inside yellowish, red-patterned, with long cilia at the edges.

S. nudiflora: blossoms purple-brown with yellow horizontal lines.

S. pillansii: blossoms dark purple-brown with purple edge cilia.

S. semota: blossoms chocolate brown with a light pattern; var. *lutea* has light-yellow flowers.

S. variegata (syn. *Orbea variegata*): the best-known species. Blossoms yellow.

Synadenium

Titanopsis

Synadenium grantii got its common name, African milk-bush, because of its white sap (latex), which flows out at the slightest injury, and which is very poisonous.

Titanopsis calcarea has wonderful, golden-yellow blossoms that shine like silk and also especially striking markings on the plant's body.

Synadenium grantii.

General notes: *Synadenium* is a genus of Euphorbiaceae from South Africa, and is related to *Euphorbia*. *S. grantii* is one cultivated species. The sprouts are round, cylindrical, green, and grow up to ¾-inch (2 cm) thick. The slightly fleshy alternate leaves are roundish, often folded, and have wavy, finely dentate edges with a reddish center rib on the genuine species. There are decorative commercial cultivars with dark-red or greenish red-speckled leaves. The small, dark-red blossoms (like the *Euphorbia* cyathia) sit on the inflorescences at the tip or in the axil of the sprouts.

Care: Location: warm, light, and in bright sun. In the winter the leaves fall off; in the summer, they only fall off in the shade. Water generously in the summer; in the winter, only a little. So that the plants will look decorative and bushy, cut them back frequently. You can put several cuttings into one pot. Propagate by cuttings or seed.

Titanopsis calcarea.

General notes: The leaves of these rosette-shaped members of the Aizoaceae are thickened sparlike or clublike towards the leaf tips; there they are densely covered with tubercles. These tubercles and the plant's color serve as camouflage in their habitat, where they grow in between the stones.

Care: Location: light and warm; best under glass. Even in the summer, water only very little. Winter temperature, 60°F (15°C). The somewhat difficult and delicate plants grow best in a sandy soil with old marble rubble mixed in. Propagate by seed.

Species: *T. calcarea:* the most beautiful species, with 3½-inch-wide (8 cm) rosettes. Leaves light-green–bluish with reddish gray-white tubercles. Golden yellow to orange blossoms. *T. fullerii:* blue-gray reddish leaves, tubercles at the edges; dark-yellow blossoms. *T. primosii:* light gray-green leaves with bubblelike tubercles; yellow flowers. *T. schwantesii:* similar to *T. primosii;* yellow flowers.

Tradescantia

Tradescantia navicularis.

General notes: Only a few species of this Central American and Peruvian genus from the spiderwort family (Commelinaceae) are leaf succulents.
Care: Hanging plants, very undemanding. Location: light, sunny, but not too hot. Winter rest period: 46°F (8°C). Water very little, never directly on the leaves. Fertilize regularly during the growth period. Easily propagated by seed or cuttings.
Species: *T. crassifolia*: a rarity with sky-blue blossoms on round, bent, hairy sprouts.
T. navicularis (chain plant): has opposite, boat-like bent-up leaves that stand above each other like roof tiles and are thick-fleshed and distinctly carinated on the back side. The leaf color is gray-green with dense violet dots; the edges carry cilia. The zigzag-shaped, creeping, short-sectioned sprouts grow rather long. Small pink blossoms stand in cymes.
T. sillamontana has white-haired leaves and pink blossoms.

Trichocaulon

Trichocaulon cactiforme.

General notes: These Asclepiadaceae from South Africa almost look like cacti, because their round, cylindrical sprouts are densely covered with soft-bristled tubercles. The small blossoms sit in multiples between the tubercles, usually at the end of the sprout.
Care: Extremely difficult, because they are constantly threatened by root rot. Water only enough that the roots do not dry out; keep absolutely dry from January to June. Location: very sunny and warm; during the winter rest period, not below 64°F (18°C). A lot of sand, perlite, and pumice in the soil; lower the pots into pumice and keep that moist. Can be grafted onto *Ceropegia woodii* or *Stapelia*.
Species: *T. clavatum* (syn. *T. cactiforme*): up to 6 inches tall (15 cm); waxy-ringed sprouts; cream-colored to yellowish blossoms with red or dark-brown dots.
T. columnare: blossoms red-speckled on the outside; on the inside, yellowish green, red-dotted, white-haired; easy to care for.

Trichodiadema

Trichodiadema barbatum.

General notes: This genus from the carpetweed family (Aizoaceae) includes low shrubs with short, slender, crooked branches and small, roundish, bristled, papillose leaves; seen through dewdrops, they glitter like a diadem. The plants need the night dew in order to survive in their native habitat.
Care: Undemanding, fast-growing, willing to bloom. Location: very sunny and airy, in the summer can be outdoors; water abundantly. Winter rest period: dry and light, above 46°F (8°C). The easy-to-care-for plants are propagated by seed or cuttings.
Species: *T. barbatum*: gray-green leaves with black bristles; blossoms deep red.
T. densum: very willing to bloom; leaves with long white bristles at the leaf tips; large, carmine-red blossoms.
T. mirabilis: cylindrical leaves with dark-brown bristles and white blossoms.
T. aureum, yellow flowers; *T. occidentalis* and *T. gracilis*, pink; *T. setuliferum* and *T. stellatum*, violet.

Of the numerous species of the genus Tradescantia, Trades-cantia navicularis shows the most distinct signs of succulence.

The cylindrical or globular stems of Trichocaulon cactiforme (syn. T. clavatum), which are 1½ to 2½ inches (4 to 6 cm) in diameter, are densely covered with tubercles.

Trichodiadema barbatum is one of 30 species, which, in their native habitat, absorb dew out of the morning air, which lets the plant glitter in the reflected light like a diadem covered with diamonds.

EXTRA TIP: *Trichodiadema densum strongly resembles Dolichothele, a genus of cactus, another case of convergence in succulents.*

Tips on Buying and Arranging Plants

The search for certain cacti and other succulents sometimes can be as exciting as the hunt for stamps. A collector swears by his suppliers for rarities that the common plant trade does not offer; however, the normal selection at plant stores, nurseries, garden centers, and even at supermarkets is plentiful and offers many possibilities for attractive plantings in bowls, pots, tubs, and troughs for indoor and outdoor use.

Terra cotta vase with cascades of Gazania and Drosanthemum.

Succulents for Indoors and Outdoors

Did the parade of the candidates for the beauty contest of cacti and other succulents stimulate you to be your own jury? Whoever wants to bring a favorite candidate into the house should consider this carefully: Beauty alone may not bring joy forever. One should consider one's own capabilities and experience as a caretaker of exotic plants; one should take the room conditions into consideration; and the realization that comes of this should be an important factor in the decisions for the selection. Although succulents in general do not have high demands concerning their care, not all are suitable for beginners.

Buying Recommendations

The first precondition for keeping them successfully is, as is the case with all plants, the purchase of healthy specimens. And this is exactly where trouble starts for an inexperienced layman. How does one know if a plant is healthy? If this is not easy, regarding the often-seen standard selections in our plant shops, it is even more difficult regarding exotic plants, whose normal, natural habitus is often totally unknown to the buyer.

Look critically at the pot and the soil. Both should have neither mold nor algae. Clean pots give reason for the assumption that the growers paid attention to plant hygiene. And, since one cannot take the plant out of the pot in the store in order to check whether the roots have rot spots or whether parasites are breeding in them, clean pots are some kind of guarantee. Spots on the fleshy leaves or bodies should cause concern. Whether caused by disease, parasites, sunburn, or whatever else, they are blemishes. The rings that can be seen on many succulents and cacti must be intact. Dried-up leaf tips, for example on agaves or aloes, should keep you from purchasing the plants. And another tip: The best guarantee that one is well-served and -advised is obtained from an expert in a succulent or cactus gardening supply store.

Succulents for Beginners

In the following box you will find recommended succulents that are suitable for beginners. They are usually offered in the stores in minipots as young plants, but they grow very rapidly.

Succulents for Small Areas

Agavaceae
Agave filifera var. compacta,
   A. maculosa, A. parviflora,
   A. pumila

Aizoaceae
Argyroderma delaetii,
   A. pearsonii
Cephalophyllum species
Cheiridopsis candidissima,
Conophytum bilobum, C. cupreatum, C. pearsonii, C. spec.
Dorotheanthus, including hybrids
Faucaria felina, F. lupina,
   F. tuberculosa,
Fenestraria aurantiaca,
Frithia pulchra
Gibbaeum dispar, G. velutinum
Glottiphyllum fragans,
   G. linguiforme
Lithops aucampiae, L. bella,
   L. bromfieldii, L. erniana,
   L. hallii, L. marmorata
Oophytum
Ophthalmophyllum praesectum
Oscularia
Pleiospilos bolusii
Rhombophyllum, all species
Ruschia uncinata
Schwantesia
Titanopsis calcarea

Asclepiadaceae
Caralluma frerei, C. hesperidum
Huernia zebrina
Stapelia variegata
Trichocaulon clavatum

Compositae
Senecio articulatus, S. kleinia

Crassulaceae
Adromischus maculatus
Crassula arta, C. barbata, C. dejecta, C. hemisphaerica,
   C. tomentosa
Dudleya farinosa
Graptopetalum filiferum ×
   Graptoveria
Kalanchoe blossfeldiana
Sedum caeruleum, S. compactum, S. palmeri

Euphorbiaceae
Euphorbia caput-medusae,
   E. horrida, E. obesa

Liliaceae
Aloe haworthioides, A. humilis,
   A. parvula, A. polyphylla,
   A. variegata
Gasteria armstrongii,
   G. liliputana, G. maculata,
   G. pulchra, G. verrucosa
Gastrolea beguinii
Haworthia bolusii, H. fasciata,
   H. reinwardtii, H. setata,
   H. truncata

Portulacaceae
Anacampseros alstonii, A. filamentosa, A. papyracea

Crassula species can develop a bizarre habitus and are easily cultivated as miniature trees in small pots. Those who want to accelerate their development can repot them into larger pots after they have been in the decorative bonsai pots for a while.

Pachypodium are robust, easy-to-care-for room plants that only dislike too much wetness and cold. Pachypodium lamerei, Pachypodium geayi, and Pachypodium saundersii are well known as potted plants.

Succulents for Outdoors

Many plant lovers have only small gardens, balconies, or terraces, but nevertheless, they do not want to do without a selection of succulents. Here, particularly *Sedum, Sempervivum* (houseleek), or smaller *Opuntia* are suited; they can be easily kept in bowls, tubs, strawberry containers, or troughs. Dwarf conifers, low grasses, or *Saxifraga* could be good neighbors in the containers. *Lewisia* and dwarf straw flowers can be planted together with *Sedum* and *Sempervivum*. When you go on vacation for several weeks, you do not have to worry about these plants. They are adapted to dry periods.

Larger succulents or plants that love dryness and heat, like *Agave* or *Yucca*, can serve as lead plants in the bed. They look very exotic when Aizoaceae are planted underneath them. Important: *Yucca* and *Agave* are not winter-hardy. In temperate climates, therefore, lower them into the ground in their pots and take them out before the first frost. Check with your local plant supplier to see if or when they need to be brought in Keep them where it is light and cool indoors during the winter. The hardiest of the Aizoaceae is, by the way, *Delosperma rubigineum* (syn. *Delosperma othonna*). It quickly covers large areas, but it can easily be cut back.

Recommended *Sedum* Species

Sedum acre var. *minus, S. album* var. *chloroticum, S. album* var. *micranthum, S. atlanticum, S. beyrichianum, S. humifusum, S. obtusatum, S. pluricaule, S. quadrifidum, S. spathulifolium, S. ternatum.*

Recommended *Sempervivum* Species

Sempervivum ballsii, S. leucanthum, S. macedonicum, S. octopodes, S. ossetiense, S. pittonii, S. pumilum, S. reginae-amaliae, S. thompsonii.

Recommended *Opuntia* Species

O. fragilis var. *fragilis, O. fragilis* var. *denuata, O. humifusa* var. *humifusa, O. phaeacantha* 'Minor,' *O.* 'Smithwick.'

Advice on Buying Cacti

What is of concern for the other succulents holds true especially for the cacti. One cannot always see at first glance if they are healthy or if they feel well. Their often dense spine or hair coat sometimes does not reveal for quite a while that they are already dead. In order to avoid that as much as possible, one should only select genera or species in which the danger of such a loss is not so high. Beginners are particularly fascinated by the flowering of cacti. They buy every cactus, hoping that they can get it to bloom. In this respect, the list of recommended species on page 128 will help to avoid disappointments, as far as possible.

An opulently planted succulents bowl.

Several Sedum and Sempervivum species are combined in this bowl, which only measures 16 inches (40 cm) in diameter. This undemanding group does not put up too much of a fight for nutrients and water; nevertheless, one should thin them out, divide them, and arrange them anew from time to time. The location for such a bowl can be a light window spot that is especially airy. In the summer, this arrangement may also be outdoors, but it must be protected from rain to avoid rotting the plants.

Succulents for Larger Areas

Agavaceae
Agave filifera, A. shawii, A. utahensis, A. victoriae-reginae

Aizoaceae
Trichodiadema densum

Apocynaceae
Adenium obesum var. *multiflorum*
Pachypodium geayi, P. lamerei, P. rutenbergerianum
Plumeria rubra

Asclepiadaceae
Ceropegia dichotoma, C. fusca, C. woodii

Commelinaceae
Tradescantia species

Compositae
Senecio crassissimus, S. haworthii, S. herreanus, S. medleywoodii, S. rowleyanus, S. scaposus, S. sempervivus, S. stapeliiformis

Crassulaceae
Aeonium arboreum, A. arboreum var. *atropurpureum, A. haworthii*
Cotyledon orbiculata, C. orbiculata var. *dinteri, C. undulata*
Crassula arborescens, C. corymbulosa, C. falcata, C. portulacea, C. pyramidalis, C. rupestris

Dudleya pulverulenta
Echeveria agavoides, E. elegans, E. leucotricha, E. laui, E. pulvinata 'Perle von Nürnberg' *and many hybrids*
Kalanchoe fedtschenkoi, K. manginii, K. pumila, K. rhombopilosa, K. tomentosa
Pachyphytum oviferum, P. bracteosum
Sedum nussbaumerianum, S. rubrotinctum, S. sempervivoides
Sempervivum tectorum and many other species

Euphorbiaceae
Euphorbia bubalina, E. grandicornis, E. polygona, E. pseudocactus, S. submammillaris, E. woodii
Monadenium coccineum
Pedilanthus tithymaloides
Synadenium grantii

Geraniceae
Pelargonium species like *P. carnosum* or *P. tetragonum*

Liliaceae
Aloe arborescens, A. aristata, A. descoingsii, A. ferox, A. variegata

Locations and Containers

Once struck by the cactus fever—and that can happen even after seeing a single, perhaps flowering cactus—a real collector's passion usually sets in. It is like stamp collecting. One can collect species or motifs—for example, only hairy species, or only leaf cacti. But one can also simply select beautiful cacti, following one's own very personal taste.

Since, except for the epiphytic species, all cacti are very hungry for light and sun, a windowsill is necessary for the positioning of the prickly treasures. Unfortunately, space at the window is always limited.

Which and how many plants can be placed there, can or should, last but not least, depend on the personal ambitions of the succulent lover. A fanatic who wants to complete his or her collection will use every possibility to make more room. Since the lighting decreases very quickly inside the room, the windowsill must not be too deep, i.e., at the most about 20 inches (50 cm). In the case of cacti that are columnar or globular, but usually don't grow over the edge of the pot, the pots can be placed densely next to each other, insofar as they are uniform as much as possible in size and shape. Four-sided pots made out of plastic are helpful. Another possibility is to lower the pots into bowls, if one does not plant directly into the bowls. This way, one can not only "hide" containers of different sizes and shapes, but also group the plants nicely. Rectangular or oval troughs made out of various materials—wood, sheet zinc, copper, brass, Styrofoam, clay or ceramics, glass, or plastic—are especially suitable for the windowsill.

The Correct Grouping

It is important that the ratio of the plant size and height to those of the container be correct. A deep container, above which the plants can barely be seen, would be disadvantageous visually. In this regard it is good that most of the cacti and other succulents have shallow roots. For larger bowls, a depth of 4 to 6 inches (10 to 15 cm) usually is sufficient. Bowls that are evenly deep are preferable to those that flatten out at the ends. But one should always pay attention to the range in heights of the plants: taller species belong at the back: i.e., towards the room. Towards the front (the window), arrange the plants in steps. Combine columns with globes and shrubby forms; that looks very effective. Ground covers that hang over the edge also look very pretty. Whether one decides on a plant arrangement of tone on tone (monotone) or on many colors depends on personal taste. Almost all ideas can be realized with cacti alone or with the other succulents alone, which generally grow faster than the cacti, or with a mixture of cacti and other succulents.

Various Easy-Blooming Cactus Species

Acanthocalycium glaucum,
    A. violaceum
Aporocactus flagelliformis,
    hybrids
Astrophytum asterias, A. capri-
    corne, A. myriostigma
Chamaecereus silvestrii
Cleistocactus vulpis-cauda
Dolichothele baumii,
    D. longimamma
Echinocereus acifer, E. dasya-
    cantha, E. fendleri, E. fitchii,
    E. hempelii, E. salm-dyckianus,
    E. pentalophus
Echinofossulocactus arrigens,
    E. crispatus, E. lamellosus,
    E. multicostatus, E. vaupelianus
Echinopsis aurea, E. kermesina,
    E. kratochviliana, E. tubiflora
    many hybrids, most with:
    Lobivia
    and Trichocereus
Epiphyllum hybrids
Gymnocalycium andreae, G.
    baldianum, G. bruchii, G. dam-
    sii, G. gibbosum, G. leeanum,
    G. mihanovichii, G.
    quehlianum
Hamatocactus setispinus
Heliocereus speciosus
Hildewintera aureispina
Hylocereus undatus
Lobivia arachnacantha, L. bing-
    hamiana, L. densispina, L. fam-
    atimensis, L. glauca,
    L. oligotricha, L. tiegeliana,
    L. westii, L. winteriana
Lophophora williamsii

Mammillaria backebergiana, M.
    bella, M. bocasana, M. brau-
    neana, M. elongata,
    M. gracilis, M. hahniana,
    M. klissingiana, M. kunzeana,
    M. longiflora, M. microhelia,
    M. mystax, M. neocoronaria,
    M. prolifera, M. schiedeana,
    M. spinosissima, M. viereckii,
    M. wildii, M. woodsii,
    M. zeilmanniana
Neoporteria atrispinosa, N. ger-
    ocephala, N. subgibbosa,
    N. villosa
Nopalxochia phyllanthoides
Notocactus concinnus, N. hasel-
    bergii, N. herteri, N. lening-
    hausii, N. mammulosus,
    N. ottonis, N. pampeanus,
    N. rutilans, N. scopa, N. tabu-
    laris, N. uebelmannianus
Opuntia azurea, O. bergeriana
Parodia chrysacanthion, P. mair-
    anana, P. mutabilis, P. nivosa,
    P. pencillata, P. procera,
    P. sanguiniflora
Rebutia (Aylostera) albiflora,
    R. deminuta, R. heliosa,
    R. kupperiana, R. marsoneri,
    R. pseudodeminuta,
    R. violaciflora
Rhipsalidopsis gaertneri, R. rosea
Schlumbergera russeliana,
    S. truncata
Selenicereus grandiflorus,
    S. pteranthus

Flowering Schlumbergera hybrids, an exciting color spectacle on the windowsill

Cactus springtime at the window.

Arrangement Suggestions

Perhaps some concrete suggestions will help you; each was meant for a container 20 inches × 8 inches (50 × 20 cm) or a bowl 12 to 14 inches (30 to 35 cm) in diameter.

Mini-Landscape in White: For the background, choose, for example, a *Cleistocactus straussii*, which should have one or two columns and be about 12 to 16 inches tall (30–40 cm). Next to it, an *Opuntia microdasys* var. *albata*, a *Cephalocereus senilis*, or an *Espostoa lanata* will have a very decorative effect. In front of this, one could maybe place a tennis-ball-sized *Astrophytum myrostigma* and two to three pretty, white-spined or white-haired *Mammillaria* (for example *Mammillaria woodsii*, *M. viereckii*, *M. bocasana*) or *Parodias*—maybe, *P. nivosa*. Also *Aylostera deminuta* would go with it very well, a species that sprouts abundantly and can grow beyond the edge of the bowl. An alternative to the prickly white would be maybe also *Cotyledon undulata* or *Senecio haworthii*—an older, branched specimen. A 12-inch-tall (30 cm) plant would be best surrounded by *Kalanchoe scapigera* or *Kalanchoe tomentosa*; in front of it *Pachyphytum oviferum*, *Crassula* 'Morgans Beauty,' *Echeveria laui*, and as "overhanger," maybe *Sedum morganianum*. The best contrast to the white plants is most effectively a plain dark bowl.

Tone-on-Tone Combinations: The bodies of cacti and also of other succulents radiate, through their spines or rings, cool blue-silver tones or warm green-gold tones. This effect can be enhanced by choosing containers that accent the coloration. For example, cacti with brown or golden spines and yellow-green succulents look beautiful in green, light-brown or cream-colored containers; the beauty of blue-silvery species comes into play in blue, snow-white, or turquoise-colored containers.

Colorful Mix: Possibly you prefer a colorful mix. For cacti, this not only refers to the overall impression of the colors, but also to the spine form and coloration. A monstrous blue-green *Cereus jamacaru*; a white-haired, red-brown spined *Oreocereus trollii*; a red-dotted *Opuntia microdasys* var. *rufida*; a white-needled globular *Mammillaria*, for example *M. klissingiana*; a golden yellow *Parodia*, maybe *P. chrysacanthion*; a deep-green *Rebutia violaciflora*; and a reddish-brown-banded *Gymnocalcium mihanovichii*, nicely arranged together make a magnificent cross-section of the cactus world.

Among the other succulents, the selection is even bigger: As a tree at the horizon of the bowl landscape, an *Aeonium arboreum* var. *atropurpureum* would be excellent, perhaps surrounded by *Euphorbia submammillaris* and *Kalanchoe tomentosa*. In the foreground, a *Faucaria*, an *Aloe aristata* or *Haworthia papillosa* with *Echeveria derenbergii* and a couple of *Lithops* could have a beauty contest. As an overhanging plant, a *Stapelia* is good.

Of course, the possibilities described for the plantings are only suggestions. With a little bit of skill and imagination, every cactus and every ever-so-plain succulent can be incorporated into an effective arrangement. The effects of each can be completely different: From cool and practical with strict geometrical column and globe shapes to playful arabesques with bizarrely wound and branched plant formations.

Decorative Oddities

Many cactus-lovers are enticed by the difficult. They want to grow species that bloom in cultivation only rarely or only at an old age, and they find especially complicated species or bizarre oddities very interesting. A small list of cacti that bloom only very rarely or very late in life follows.

Austrocephalocereus dybowskii
Borzicactus icosagonus, B. samaipatanus
Cephalocereus senilis
Cereus peruvianus, C. jamacaru; monstrous forms
Cleistocactus straussii
Echinocactus grusonii, E. horizonthalonius, E. ingens
Echinocereus pectinatus var. *rigidissimus,* var. *rubrispinus*
Espostoa lanata, E. melanostele, E. nana
Eulychnia saint-pieana, E. spinibarbis
Ferocactus glaucescens, F. latispinus, F. robustus, F. wislizeni
Haageocereus albispinus, versicolor
Lemaireocereus thurberi
Leuchtenbergia principis
Myrtillocactus geometrizans
Notocactus magnificus
Opuntia clavarioides (Austrocylindropuntia), O. microdasys with varieties, *O. rufida*
Oreocereus celsianus, O. fossulatus, O. maximus, O. trollii
Pilosocereus pachycladus, P. rosalensis
Stetsonia coryne

Tone-on-tone combinations.

Silver-blue combination. In the approximately 13 × 8¾-inch (33 × 22 cm) oval, blue-glazed bonsai dish are two fine specimens of the pink-blooming Mammillaria kunthii, as well as several small, blue-ringed succulents. To cover up the soil, little snow-white pebbles were used.

A brown-green-gold-combination. The bowl, only 8¾ × 6½ × 2½ inches (22 × 16 × 6 cm), houses an Opuntia as well as Brasilicactus haselbergii and Mammillaria. To cover the soil, little beige-colored stones were chosen. The decorative figurines, which, like the cacti, originate in America, are very pretty with it.

Formation of the Soil Surface

The character of the composition created by the bowl and the plants can be enhanced by the formation of the soil surface. It is in any case suggested that you cover up the actual roots. It not only looks nicer, it also has advantages when you water. Potential materials are: sand, round pebbles, angular stone chips, potsherds, charcoal, tile chips, absorbent clay, glass pearls, and more. Except for the sand, the particles can range from 1⁄8-inch to 1¼ inches (a few millimeters to several centimeters). You may cover up the soil in one color, or you may set parts of the surface by using different materials and colors. With natural minerals, such as light-colored limestone, dark granite, reddish porphyry pebbles, and yellow or white sand, it is possible to imitate nature. Or should the taste of the 1950s be revived? Cactus pebbles can be bought in all colors. Whether this is "kitsch" is debatable, as is the use of garden dwarfs. Children, anyway, find a colorfully pebbled little succulent bowl cute and funny. So that the differently-colored pebbles do not get mixed up when one waters, it is suggested that you spray the pebble layer with a clear gloss enamel. The little stones then stick together.

Bowl, plants, and soil covering should be in harmony with each other, but they may also contrast. Brown absorbent clay looks better in a light bowl than in a dark one; with sand it is exactly the opposite. A coarse granulation requires a certain plant size. A calm sand surface is enlivened by a rocky, bizarre, knotty root

Cacti that are freely planted out directly in the soil can develop by far more splendidly than those kept in pots. The location in a winter garden with light from all sides contributes to the development of intense colors in the red, golden, silver, or brown spines.

that would appear lost on coarse pebbles. Give free play to your imagination and taste.

As pretty as containers may be to look at, you cannot expect to be able to enjoy them unchanged for years. The other succulents, even more than the cacti, grow luxuriantly and cannot be kept for too long in the desired form and size. Therefore, you will have to be prepared to replant them.

Succulents Planted Outside

The basic rules that apply to a container arrangement also apply to landscape creations in a window or winter garden. Whether the microclimate of such a place is at all salubrious to succulents depends on its location and equipment. Bad ventilation and bad heating possibilities, and thus too high air humidity would be problematic (except for epiphytic species). It would be preferable to lower potted plants into the ground instead of planting them freely out into ground or table beds. Since the light outdoors does not fall from one side only, but from above, one can arrange the plants solely by the way they look. If there is enough space, one should place several specimens of the same species or genus, but also sometimes larger and smaller ones, together in groups. There must remain enough free space, though; only then the unusual habitus of the exotic beauties will come into play to its full extent.

Solitary Plants

And now a word about solitary plants, which can be something special for every indoor gardener. In the plant

business, there are *Euphorbia* available, for example, *E. canariensis, E. candelabrum, E. cooperi, E. milii,* with numerous varieties, *E. grandicornis* or *E. trigona;* also *Aeonium arboreum* varieties. *Pachypodium lamerei,* which can be brought as a cute little "palm tree," and which can grow after several years into an impressive, exotic accent in front of the sunny window wall, has become almost a fancy plant. More and more often, these plants are also offered in hydroculture. An unusual leaf plant that looks impressive is *Kalanchoe beharensis,* velvetleaf. One hardly needs to mention the indestructibility of a *Sansevieria*—especially in unfavorable, shady locations. The *Sansevieria* (bowstring hemp), which, by the way, quickly fills large containers, displays the entire beauty of its leaf markings only in the sun. One must not forget magnificent *Agave* species—for example, *A. victoriae-reginae, A. utahensis,* or *A. americana,* which always enrich terraces and balconies in the summer as tub plants and can add green color during the winter to a cool, light stairway.

Succulents for Hanging Arrangements

Some succulents are suitable for use as interesting, alternative hanging plant arrangements, for example: *Sedum morganianum, Senecio radicans, Kalanchoe uniflora, Kalanchoe pumila, Ceropegia woodii, Crassula perforata,* and *Crassula socialis,* not to mention the magnificently blooming epiphytic cacti.

Cacti planted directly in the ground.

Winter-Blooming Succulents			
Species	Flowers in	Blossoms	Space
Aeonium arboreum var. atropurpureum	January/February	Golden yellow	Wide
A. cunatum	January/February	Light yellow	Wide
A. gomerense	January/February	Ochre	Wide
A. hierrense	January/February	Light pink	Wide
A. urbicum	January/February	White, greenish, or pinkish	Wide
Aloe albiflora	December/March	Pure white	Narrow, also needs little sun
A. arborescens	November/January	Bright red	Wide
A. haworthioides	November/January	Pale orange	Wide
A. saponaria	November/January	Red-yellow	Wide
A. squarrosa	January/February	Red	Narrow
A. variegata	January/February	Light vermilion	Wide
Crassula albiflora	From November on	White	Narrow
C. columnaria	From November on	White to yellowish orange	Narrow
C. cooperi	From November on	Flesh color	Narrow
C. lactea	From November on	White	Wide
C. mesembryan-themopsis	From November on	White	Narrow
C. 'Morgan's Beauty'	February/March	Pink	Narrow
C. rupestris	From November on	Yellow or White to pink	Narrow
Echeveria carnicolor	From November/December	Orange	Narrow
E. derenbergii	January/April	Reddish yellow to yellow	Narrow
E. elegans	January/April	Reddish yellow	Narrow
Graptopetalum paraguayense	From February on	Yellowish white	Narrow
Kalanchoe blossfeldiana	January/March	Scarlet-red	Wide
K. daigremontiana	January/March	Gray-violet	Wide
K. laxiflora	January/March	Pink-orange	Wide
K. peteri	January/April	Pale-yellow	Wide
K. pumila	January/April	Reddish-violet	Wide
K. tubiflora	Janury/March	Orange to violet	Wide
K. uniflora	January/March	Red	Hanging
Pachyphytum oviferum	From January on	Greenish-white	Narrow
Sedum adolphii	January/April	White	Wide
S. bellum	January/April	White	Hanging
S. nussbaumerianum	January/April	White	Wide
S. pachyphyllum	January/April	Yellow	Wide
S. palmeri	January/April	Orange-yellow	Wide
S. rubrotinctum	January/April	Yellow	Wide
S. stahlii	January/April	Yellowish green	Hanging
S. treleasei	January/April	Light yellow	Wide
Senecio barbertonensis	February/April	Golden yellow	Wide
S. medley-woodii	January/April	Yellow	Wide
S. radicans	From December	White with yellow to light purple anthers	Hanging
S. rowleyanus	From November	White with brown-violet anthers	Hanging
S. spiculosus	December/March	White	Wide

The Epiphyllum hybrids 'Masada' and 'American Sweetheart' are kept in hanging pots. They bloom abundantly and they are eyecatchers and attractions of every winter garden or greenhouse.

Flowering Time of Succulents

Did you know that there are numerous winter bloomers among the succulents? The table to the left lists some examples.

Flowering Time of Cacti

To make a flowering calendar for cacti seems risky, because the flowering time not only varies from year to year, but also depends to a considerable degree on the way they are cultivated. Besides, the flowering times of the individual species of the same genus are to some extent spread out over a long period of time. Here is a small list as a guide:

These bloom from February through May: *Aporocactus, Astrophytum, Echinocereus fitchii, Echinofossulocactus, Echinopsis, Epiphyllum, Gymnocalycium bruchii, Mammillaria viereckii, M. woodsii, M. wildii, M. zeilmanniana, Notocactus, Nopalxochia, Parodia chrysacanthion, Rebutia, Rhipsalidopsis gaertneri.*

In June and July: *Acanthocalycium, Aylostera, Blossfeldia, Coryphantha, Dolichothele, Echinocactus, Echinocereus, Frailea, Gymnocalycium leeanum, Hamatocactus, Lobivia, Mammillaria neocoronaria, M. spinosissima, Neoporteria, Opuntia, Parodia mairanana, Selenicereus.*

From August through October: *Gymnocalycium mihanovichii, Hamatocactus setispinus, Leuchtenbergia principis, Mammillaria plumosa, M. schiedeana, Parodia hausteiniana.*

From November through January: *Rhipsalis* and other epiphytes, *Schlumbergera* and its hybrids, and *Zygocactus.*

Epiphyllum hybrids in a greenhouse.

Successful Care and Propagation

It is not difficult to successfully care for succulents, to propagate them, and to bring them to bloom again and again. Nevertheless, the plant lover will not be able to do this entirely without guidelines. After all, we are dealing with exotic guests that have to adapt their individual life rhythms to our light and climate conditions. We can help them with this and save them from diseases and parasites. In the following chapter, you will learn everything that is important about the correct soil, light, air, watering, fertilizing, the winter rest period, and about plant protection. Anyone who wants to sow cacti from seed or wants to propagate them in another way will find guidelines that can be followed easily—as well as notes for the *haute école* of grafting.

In the greenhouse, cacti have an optimal location and can get plenty of light for blossom formation.

Essential Factors in Care

In caring for succulents, we strive to come as close as possible to the conditions in their native habitats. Thanks to the high capacity for adaption of these exotics, this task is made a lot easier for the amateur gardener.

Light, the Vital Element

Cacti and other succulents are for the most part children of the light. Light influences growth and blossom formation positively and helps their spines to develop more intense coloration. Almost all succulents love the light and sun during their growth periods, but this is particularly true of all very hairy, heavily spined, and white-ringed species. In the spring, though, they have to get used to the light; in the summer they have to be protected from the full noonday sun. The leaf cacti, Christmas and Easter cacti, *Gasteria*, or *Haworthia*, and also *Echinopsis*, *Gymnocalycium*, green *Mammillaria* and *Cereus* like it less sunny, but very light.

Leaf cacti like hybrids of *Epiphyllum* and *Nopalxochia*, *Rhipsalidopsis*, and *Schlumbergera* like light, half-shady, evenly humid, warm locations and, in the summer, a place in the half-shade.

Very specific amounts of daily light influence the rest period, as well as the flowering of the succulents. Short-day plants like *Kalanchoe blossfeldiana* and the Christmas cactus, *Schlumbergera*, need 4 to 6 weeks of short light and long dark periods in the fall, in order to be able to form blossoms. Long-day plants like *Sedum* species need long daily light periods and short dark periods. Some species like mixed time periods—for example *Kalanchoe crenatum* or *Senecio* species.

On dark days during the months with little light (or in the winter rest period in a dark basement) one can also prolong and enhance the daylight with special grow-lights (available in plant stores). High-intensity mercury lamps are very suitable. Important: the lamps should always be installed by an expert, and ask for a timer, because, after all, the lamps are not supposed to be on all the time. Buy only plant lights that are waterproofed so they won't be affected by watering.

Air and Temperature

All succulents love a lot of fresh and clean air; in the fall and winter it should be draft-free and temperature-controlled. They do not take tobacco smoke well! Dry room air, on the other hand, is tolerated.

At summery temperatures of 86° to 95°F (30° to 35°C) or more, the room has to be aired out, i.e., the accumulated heat has to be pushed out, and it is necessary to provide shade and to water well. If the temperature drops at night to 64° to 68°F (18° to 20°C), it does not do any damage. Ground temperature of about 77°F (25°C) in the spring is helpful. If the plants are on cool stone windowsills, place heating mats (available from plant stores) underneath.

Many succulents from foggy deserts between the coast and high mountains love to be sprinkled, which is perceived by them as if it were native dew. Important: On warm summer and fall days sprinkle them; but only with soft water at room temperature. Make sure that the plant body is dry before the temperature drops.

Winter Resting Period

The general rule is that in the winter cacti should be kept at a temperature of no more than 41° to 46°F (5° to 8°C); the other succulents at a temperature of no more than 50° to 54°F (10° to 12°C), and they always should be kept light and dry, because otherwise they may not bloom.

Only *Euphorbia milii*, *Pilosocereus*, *Haageocereus*, *Melocactus*, *Discocactus* and some *Opuntia* are kept warmer during the winter. *Echinocereus*, *Echinopsis*, *Lobivia*, *Opuntia*, and *Rebutia* like to be kept colder than described above.

Anyone who does not have a light place for the winter rest period can, if need be, keep some genera, like *Lobivia*, *Rebutia*, or *Notocactus*, in a dark place in the winter. But it is better to use grow-lamps as a helping device at such less-optimal winter rest locations. Important: One has to get the plants slowly used to the stronger light in the spring.

Opuntia fragilis, here planted directly in the ground in a sunny stone garden, are among the winter-hardy species of the genus and unfold numerous bright yellow blossoms.

Winter-hardy Opuntia fragilis.

Suitable Locations

Most succulents are not kept outdoors. Only the hardy *Sedum* and *Sempervivum* species and certain *Agave*, *Aloe*, and *Crassula*, as well as some *Opuntia*, *Echinocereus*, *Chamaecereus*, *Coryphanthes*, *Escobaria* are winter-hardy in Germany. Check with your local plant supplier to ascertain winter-hardiness of the above in your area. For indoor cultivation, light windowsills (in the afternoon without full sun) facing southwest or southeast are well-suited. Provide shade at true southern exposures. At 39 inches (1 m) from the window, the light has only 50% to 80% of its intensity in comparison to being directly at the window; at 6½ feet (2 m), only 10% to 24%.

It's possible to surround or cover a balcony with metal foil or glass, or even to heat it. Garden owners can put up a greenhouse of wood, metal or plastic (covered with glass, foil, or panels), with more or less technically sophisticated equipment, even highly recommended automatic heating, ventilation, and shade-providing systems. Heating costs can be considerably reduced by heat-retaining double- or multiple-layered windows, by attaching foil underneath the glass, by attaching Styrofoam inside the standing walls up to the height of a table, and by shade devices that are pulled shut at night. Draftless ventilation has to be provided constantly, even on cold days.

In the greenhouse, not only Rhipsalis (here R. houlletiana, planted in hanging pots) feels well. The greenhouse is an ideal location for all succulents, when the roof lets a lot of light come through and when it is well insulated.

The Right Soil

The demands upon the soil are low. Cacti and a number of other succulents want soil that is low in or free of humus; porous in regard to water and air; and mineral, with a lot of nutrient salts. For cultivation, you may use the excellent ready-mixed cactus soils, or soil that you mix yourself out of not-too-fine clean-washed sand with loam or clay to a pH-value about 5.5 to 6.9, and additional substances [particle size of ⅛- to ¼-inch (2 to 16 mm)], e.g. absorbent clay (used in hydroculture) and other granulated clays, pumice stone, lava grit, charcoal, perlite, tile gravel, and plastic products. Epiphytic cacti and some other succulents (e.g., Crassulaceae) want in addition a portion of humus and peat. Always provide good drainage out of pebbles, absorbent clay, or Styrofoam flakes.

Watering Correctly

Keep plants rather drier than too wet. In the summer, in sunny weather, according to their needs, one waters about once a week with lukewarm water, penetratingly ("powerfully or not at all"), in the late afternoon. In the winter, especially below 50°F (10°C), most of the time one does not water at all if it is the plant's resting period. Exceptions are the leaf cacti and those other succulents that have their rest period in the spring and summer. After each dry period, the plants have to get used to more water slowly; before each dry period, they have to get used to less water.

For the plants' optimal health, water the soil surface exactly at the edge of the pot, if possible without moistening the plant body, especially in the case of waxy-ringed or white-haired ones. For individual pots, trays are necessary. Avoid overly damp soil because of poor drainage. The simplest way still remains watering overhead. Tap water that is low on calcium and soft to medium-hard avoids calcium spots on the plants and changes the acidity of the soil very little. Rainwater today is mostly unsuitable. Hard water should be softened with ion-exchange or household water-softener devices. In addition to even ground moisture, air humidity is especially important for the epiphytes; 50% to 60% relative air humidity is sufficient in the summer and 40% to 50% in the winter for most.

Fertilizing Correctly

From the late spring to the early fall, succulents constantly need nutrients. As a rule, fertilize every 2 to 3 weeks; always only onto the moist root balls and on warm, cloudy days. Fertilize with a lower dose (0.05%) and more often, rather than with a higher dose and less frequently. Depot fertilizers with time-release effects, special cactus fertilizers, and chloride-free full fertilizers are especially suitable.

So-called leaf fertilizers, which are soluble, low in nitrogen and physiologically acid, are recommended. In the spring, and after having replanted, water several times with pure water before fertilizer is added. In late summer, or if the plants have a disease, do not fertilize anymore. If plants are to be kept intentionally small, reduce the nutrient supplements to once a month at the most.

Rhipsalis in the greenhouse.

Repotting Correctly

Regular repotting furthers the healthy development of succulents. Fast-growing succulents must be replanted once a year; most of the cacti, every 2 to 3 years. The older a plant is, the longer the intervals can get. Old plants are less tolerant of damage to the roots. For them it is sufficient to loosen up the moldy, crusty soil surface and perhaps to renew it. By the way: Fertilizing does not replace repotting (see also p. 146).

Suitable Plant Containers

Clay pots are not recommended unless lined with a peat-sand mix, except for highly succulent plants—for example, Aizoaceae, which are especially sensitive to wetness, and which are better lowered into the ground. In clay pots, the nutrients are more likely to be washed to the inside edge of the pot, so that the roots grow in this direction and, as a result, a compact root ball cannot develop. Clay pots are more stable than plastic pots (because of their weight). In the case of tall columnar cacti, which easily tip over in plastic pots, clay is more practical.

Plastic pots are useful because they do not grow algae and because they are lightweight. Their smooth surface does not let any water go through, evaporation is less, and watering can be reduced. The nutrients spread out here more evenly in the soil; thus, the root ball develops better.

When repotting, the new pot or trough should be about ¾-inch (2 cm) larger than the plant's diameter in each dimension and must have drainage holes. Many plants (especially column

Mammillaria, because of their willingness to flower, are among the most popular cacti for beginners. They can be very easily grown from seed or cuttings, and they are propagated in cactus gardens in large numbers.

cacti) can be grown very well in boxes or bowls made out of plastic, glass or wood. For sowing seed or growing of cuttings, use shallow Styrofoam containers. Even more suitable are heatable cultivation frames (available from plant stores). They supply ground warmth for successful sprouting.

For large plants, containers made of stoneware are suitable, as well as terra cotta troughs, wooden tubs, and tree-nursery containers made out of plastic. Wooden tubs should only be made with environmentally friendly chemicals that are not damaging to the plant. Outdoor succulents may be planted in stone or wooden troughs.

Succulents in Hydroculture

Although one might not think so because they are xerophytes, many succulents are nevertheless suitable for hydroculture. It is best to take cuttings and young plants that have grown roots already on substrates without soil and place them in the water at a depth so that the stem base is not below the surface of the water. In the winter rest period from November to March, the water level is reduced to a minimum; when the temperature has dropped, the water is emptied out completely. Epiphytes are especially recommended for hydroculture, but also globular and columnlike cacti, as well as *Opuntia*. More about hydroculture on page 147.

Different Methods of Propagation

There are several ways to get new plants, including propagation by seed and propagation from plant parts, also

called vegetative reproduction. In propagation by seeds, genetically unknown offspring may be created by blending of the genotypes of the parent plants; however, the young plants made by vegetative reproduction through segmentation, plantlets, cuttings, or leaf pieces will look exactly like the mother plant and share the same genetic inheritance.

In the case of succulents, propagation with plantlets, cuttings of runners or sprouts, or by segmentation is possible. Some succulents, for example *Kalanchoe pinnata*, *K. daigremontiana*, form small plantlets at the leaf edges that are already equipped with fine roots, which fall off or break off easily; placed in the soil, they grow without problems. On other succulents, runners arise at the roots, which can be separated and cultivated independently as new plants. On cacti, (for example *Echinopsis*), and also on other succulents (for example *Agave*, *Aloe*), the formation of new little sprouts at the base of the stem or higher is relatively frequent.

An offset is separated with a sharp knife from the mother plant; the cut area is sprinkled with charcoal powder, and the plant grower then continues to treat it like a cutting. With plants that grow with multiple sprouts, for example *Lobivia*, *Mammillaria*, or *Gymnocalycium*, one can use a similar procedure. Take them out of the pot and, after the dirt has been emptied, divide them from the side sprouts. In another method of propagation, the main crown of a plant is removed. The separated crown then can be treated as a cutting.

Mammillaria propagation.

Propagation by Cuttings

Parts of the plant that grow above the ground that are removed for the purpose off propagation are called cuttings. These may be head cuttings (for example in *Euphorbia*) and cuttings of the main stem, or partial cuttings without shoot tips. Leaves also can be suitable for making very productive cuttings. Even tubercles of long-tubercled *Mammillaria* or of *Leuchtenbergia principis* serve for propagation.

The top–bottom orientation of the cutting should always remain the same. Through a bevel of the cutting edges, marks the lower end (for center stem cuttings); the lower end later will grow roots in the soil. Cuttings should be cut off only if they are at least 1 inch (3 cm) long and should only be taken from healthy plants. They should be cut from young, juicy tissue; if need be, all year round. Let *Euphorbia* cuttings release their latex and callous over before rooting.

The best thing is to cut cuttings off nonblooming plants in the early summer, always in the early afternoon. Sprout parts that are blooming or want to bloom do not easily grow roots. The same holds true for cuttings from resting or sick plants.

After the cutting is severed with a sterile razor blade, the cut end is dipped about ⅜-inch (1 cm) deep into charcoal powder and is placed at least 8 to 10 days (or longer) vertically in the light, so that its sectioned area can dry. Sometimes, air roots will be created on the side which that turned away from the light after this time.

Roots may then be grown by placing the cutting in a peat–sand or sand–perlite mixture (ratios of 1:1 and 1:2, respectively), which have to be kept moist, but not wet. The cuttings are only placed onto it, or at the most lowered up to ³⁄₁₆-inch (1 to 5 mm) into the soil mixture. Leaf cacti and some other succulents are exceptions to this. The leaves should be slightly inserted into the mixture in an upright position with the leaf's upper side facing upwards. They should be taken with growth buds intact. Soil warmth furthers the formation of roots; 64° to 73°F (18° to 23°C) is optimal. Root formation can take days or months, depending on the species. When sufficient roots have grown, repot the plant and continue to care for it in the normal way.

How to Sow Succulents from Seed

The best time for sowing is spring, but for numerous South African succulents it is the fall. In the fall, additional light is necessary.

The seeds should be treated for mycosis and animal parasites with the usual available dry and wet mordants. The seedbed soil (for example, sandy cactus soil or peat–sand–perlite mixtures) should not contain any organisms that are harmful to plants so sterilize it by heating. Bowls, pots and glass plates should be cleaned thoroughly and disinfected with hot soapsuds before the seeds are sown. Later on, the seedlings should be hardened in fresh air and protected against damping off with a fungicide. After 6 to 12 months, depending on growth, seedlings should be separated and planted out into pots. Make sure that the top of the roots is at the same height as it was in the soil surface previously.

The Art of Grafting

Many succulents grow very slowly in cultivation, flower late, or are difficult to care for overall. These, and also cactus color mutations, cristate forms, and plants that are endangered by diseases, may be grafted.

In grafting, the section cut from the sensitive plant (scion) is placed onto the cut lower half of a strong-growing, undemanding base plant (stock).

Strongly sprouting stocks cause the scions to degenerate. Bases that are too weak, on the other hand, are sucked out by the scion prematurely and die. Stock and scion have to be matched regarding their genus characteristics. Some species, for example some *Opuntia*, are best suited for grafting among themselves.

Genuine, permanent stocks are cacti that grow well, like *Echinopsis*, *Eriocereus*, *Selenicereus*, and *Trichocereus* species, but also *Pereskia*, and *Rhodocactus* (for Christmas and Easter cacti) and *Pereskiopsis* species (for seedling grafting).

For the other succulents (*Euphorbia*, *Pachypodium*, Crassulaceae), the partners are usually from the same genus. The stock of *Ceropegia* species are well-suited to frequently-grafted *Stapelia*, *Hoodia*, and *Travaresia* that otherwise grow very poorly.

Moisture, soil, and fertilizer needs are determined by the stock, and light and warmth demands determined on the other hand, more by the scion.

Lithops (living stones) can be easily propagated by seed. Sow them in containers filled with a sandy cactus soil. Keep the containers warm. Sprouting takes place after 6 to 12 weeks.

Lithops propagation.

Methods of Plant Care

On the previous pages, you learned everything that is important about soil, light, air, watering, fertilizing, and overwintering of cacti and other succulents. Here are some additional tips regarding the repotting and watering of the prickly fellows.

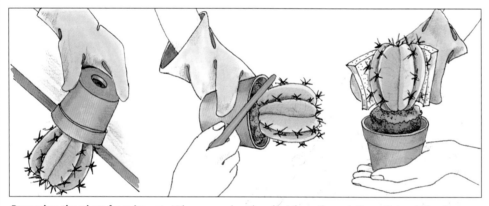

Removing the plant from its pot. *When removing the plant from the pot, the soil should be dry. So that the root ball comes loose easily, tap the edge of the inverted clay pot against the edge of a table. A plastic pot (center drawing) may be squeezed together a bit for this purpose; loosen the compressed soil with the help of a transplanting stick at the edge of the pot. After that, lift the plant out of the pot with the help of styrofoam pieces, and try to protect and preserve the roots.*

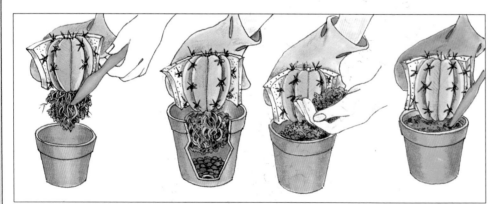

Repotting. *Shake off the old soil. Loosen the root ball with a little wooden stick or transplanting stick. For drainage, place potsherds, absorbent clay, or coarse pebbles in bottom of the pot and put a piece of fleece over them. Spread out some soil onto it; place the plant in the center of the pot, and fill in the rest of the soil in such a way that the plant sits in the new pot at the same height as in the old one. Don't forget to leave a finger-wide gap around the edges for watering.*

Repotting

Repotting is necessary when the pot becomes too small and the roots protrude from the bottom holes, when the growth stops, when the plant's willingness to bloom declines, when the green of the plant body fades, or when the soil doesn't appear to be in good condition anymore. The best time to repot is the spring and the beginning of the summer. Plants that have been attacked by parasites can be replanted until the late summer, but they must have recovered by October for overwintering. During the winter rest period, do not repot under any circumstances. Fast-growing species should be repotted every 1 to 2 years; slower-growing ones, every 2 to 3 years.

The spines are the most difficult problem. Wear thick gardening gloves. For specimens with strong spines and those with barbs, use in addition Styrofoam pieces, strong cuffs made out of newspaper, or foam-rubber strips to grab the plant. To move or replace the replanted pots, there are pot pliers available. If there is nothing else available, a piece of corrugated cardboard or a thick layer of paper will also do.

When you take the plant out of the pot, its soil should be dry, so that the root ball is easily loosened from the container. If the soil is very hard, the pot may have to be sacrificed. Smash clay pots; cut open plastic ones. The new pot should be somewhat wider than the old one, so that you can create a sufficiently wide gap for watering. Plants with storage roots require a deep pot. So that room is made for the new soil and the plant is enticed to form new roots again, matted roots have to be loosened, and it is absolutely necessary to cut off discolored or rotting roots. For disinfection, sprinkle charcoal powder onto the cut edges. The old and used earth should be discarded.

Drainage, especially in the case of succulents, is of utmost importance, because it prevents excess soil moisture. Provide drainage with material that lets water filter through (potsherds, gravel, pebbles, absorbent clay) in the bottom of the pot above the drainage hole, or, in the case of plants that are sensitive to wetness, in the area around the root neck.

In the new, clean plant container, which should be ¾-inch (2 cm) larger in each direction than the previous one, place the drainage material above the drainage holes. Then, fill in the new soil around the roots of the plant, which you hold in the center pot. Tapping the pot against the worktable compacts the soil and slightly pushes it in. The plant should stand neither higher nor deeper than in its previous pot. Leave a gap for watering around the edge.

After they are repotted, succulent plants must not be watered for about 8 days and must not be fertilized for some weeks. So that they can grow roots without stress, they should be placed in a bright spot, but not in the full sun.

Vacation Watering

Mechanized "plant-sitters" are only necessary if you go away for several weeks. Important: Check before your trip to see that the water supply in the storage vessel is sufficient for the anticipated time period.

Watering correctly. When watering from above, it is best not to moisten the plant body. It is also possible to water from the saucer. In both cases, it is absolutely necessary to pour out the extra water after 30 minutes. Otherwise there is danger of rotting.

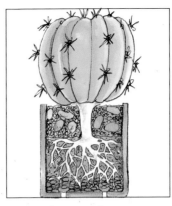

Avoid soil wetness from poor drainage. Succulents with an especially wetness-sensitive, easily rotting root neck should have, between the foundation and the surface soil, a water-conducting layer of pebbles, pumice-stone, perlite or absorbent clay, which allows the water to pass through.

Vacation watering. In a garden supply store, you can buy wicks, fleece mats, clay balls, and other "plant-sitters," which can be stuck into the soil and which by capillary action suck water out of a water-storage vessel in case the root balls become too dry while you are away. Anyone who wants to supply several pots at once may stick wicks into the pots, place them on a fleece mat, whose end reaches into a water-storage vessel, and place the pots in peat or absorbent clay.

Hydroculture. Succulents growing roots in a mineral substrate develop very well in special cultivation pots with granulated clay. The water meter (center) may only be up to "optimum" level in the summer and has to be at "minimum" for 3 days before one adds more water.

Different Methods of Propagation

The propagation of cacti and other succulents is exciting, not too difficult, and is especially recommended when you desire certain rarities that are readily available commercially. There are different ways to get new plants: sexual reproduction from seed, or vegetative reproduction from cuttings and the *haute école* of grafting.

Sowing Seed

Sexual reproduction results in seed. To sow them sieve the top layer of the soil to a depth of about ⅝-inch (1.5 cm), using a mesh of width about 0.04 inch (1 mm) and level it. If you want to grow several different kinds of seed, divide the surface, according to need, into sections with glass or plastic strips. Since it takes a long time until one can distinguish genera or species in young plants, do not forget to place a label next to the seeds, on which the name of the plant and the date of the sowing is written. The seeds, which should be spread out loosely and as evenly as possible, should only be pressed down, but not covered with soil, because, with only very few exceptions, succulents are light germinators. The seed pots must be kept saturated with water from below. The germinating temperature should be between 68° and 86°F (20° to 30°C); the air humidity should be kept high and under all circumstances the seedlings should not be allowed to dry out. Therefore, cover the seed pots with a piece of plate glass, for example, which is placed on the container at a slight angle with the help of wedges placed underneath, so that the condensed water can run off. A seedling box with a heating cable and thermostat is especially effective; it can also be easily homemade. One has to provide protection from the full sun. The seeds germinate in 3 to 21 days. Certain species, for example, *Tephrocactus*, are frost-germinators, i.e., the seeds have to be exposed to freezing temperatures for several weeks before they are planted.

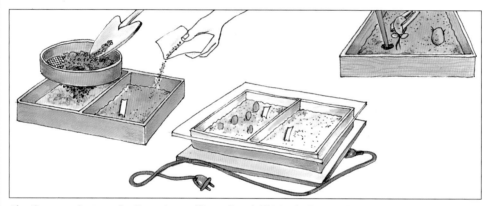

Planting succulent seeds. *Sieve the seedling soil and fill it in shallow seed pots. Let the seeds trickle onto the soil surface from a folded piece of paper. Moisten the soil by placing the seed pots in a larger container with cool boiled water. Stick identifying labels in the soil and place a heating mat underneath. Place a glass plate on top. Put the container in a bright, but not too sunny spot. As soon as the seedlings are big enough, transplant them. Carefully place them individually into a box at a distance of about ¾-inch (2 cm) or more apart.*

Leaf cuttings grow roots relatively quickly. *Separate them from the mother plant, let them dry for 1–2 days, and stick them slightly at an angle into the propagation soil. If they get the necessary warmth and moisture, they grow roots rapidly and within a few months form little rosettes.*

Plantlets *like those shown here on Kalanchoe pinnata (Mexican love plant) already have their own roots and will begin to grow in the soil immediately.*

Cuttings

Vegetative reproduction using plant parts like cuttings, leaves, or shoot tips is usually less complicated and faster than growing from seed. For most species, it is successful without great effort. Cuttings grow roots within a few weeks. Depending on the size, within a few months, you have a plant that is capable of blooming.

Grafting

In grafting succulents, only use plants of the same botanical family (e.g., Crassulaceae, Aizoaceae). In the first method, the two partners are cut horizontally and, after the edges of both parts are bevelled, the grafted plant (scion) is placed on the base (stock) so that the vascular tissue bundles of both are aligned or at least overlap. The scion should not be too small, withered, or incompatible with the stock. In a second method of grafting, the stump of the stock has a wedge removed from it and the scion has a matching point cut in it. The two are then placed together. The contact between the partners should be as tight as possible, which is achieved by placing weights on the top for 6 to 8 days, creating tension with loose rubberbands, or, for the second method, winding raffia around the cut area. Keep the scion warm and shaded until they join. Water the stock from below.

The sectioned surfaces must not come in contact with water until they have grown together for about 14 days. Do your grafts during the time of the plant's main growth; in emergencies, you may do them at any time of year, but always keep the grafted plant under glass.

The flat stem pads of the Opuntia are ideal for making cuttings.

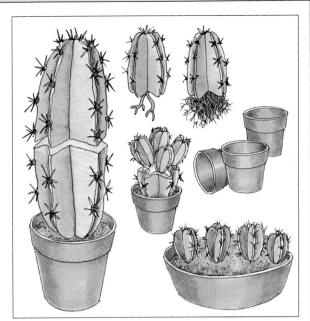

While the crown of the plant grows roots, the stump grows sprouts—a source of new cuttings.

A robust one-stemmed stock, coinciding in its cross-section with that of the scion as much as possible, is cut horizontally between last year's and this year's growth zone. The cut edges of the scion and the stock are bevelled; the scion is placed on the stock with vascular tissue bundles aligned. The pieces, held together with rubber bands, join in about 14 days.

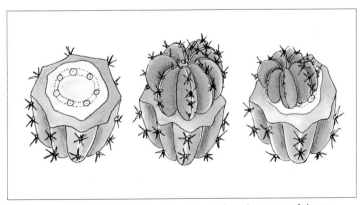

If the scion is smaller in diameter than the stock, at least one of the vascular tissue bundle rings, or even one single bundle, has to be aligned on both. The eccentric scion usually grows again later on.

Protection for Succulents

Succulents are robust and not very susceptible to parasites, fungi, viruses, and bacteria. But even with the most optimal, well-balanced, and toughening care, diseases and parasites occur. But, the stronger and faster-growing a plant is, the better it can deal with it. Besides optimal care, one can use quite a few of other preventive measures.

Preventive Measures

One of the most important preventive measures is to avoid mistakes in care. Especially in the case of the highly succulent species, one can do a lot of damage by overly generous watering. Also a too warm or too dark winter rest period can be the cause of infectious diseases, because it makes the plant tissue limp and susceptible. An important preventive measure is optimal hygiene. Dried out, rotted, or sick plant material always has to be removed; all cut areas should be sprinkled with charcoal powder for disinfection. Keep pots and soil clean. Remove algae and moss regularly and check on your plants at brief intervals. The earlier one discovers evil-doers like lice or mites, the more easily they can be fought.

Weapon Choices

There are a number of choices for effectively fighting parasites and diseases of cacti and other succulents listed below:

Biotechnical measures like yellow cards with adhesive on them should be only used indoors, outdoors, unfortunately, beneficial insects also will stick to them.

Biological control measures like useful insects or preparations that contain plant-derived insecticides like pyrethrum.

Chemicals like insecticides, fungicides or acaricides (mite-killing preparations). In some countries, there are no measures permitted to kill bacteria, and nothing is available against viruses. Oil-containing mediums (e.g., paraffin oil) and soap-like mediums, for example based on the potash salts of natural fatty acids, belong to the group of the chemical control mediums. Chemical poisons should, for environmental protection reasons, be used only in emergencies, i.e., in cases of very strong attacks or with very old, valuable, irreplaceable plants. Attention: Highly poisonous chemicals do not belong in the hands of a layman.

Biological Protection

The first step in the fight is the removal of the damaged or sick plant parts, as well as the removal of the pests. In the case of prickly specimens, this can be done with a pair of tweezers or with a wooden stick. After that, control, following the principles of the integrated plant protection, should have priority. It is followed by using biological means like pyrethrum, derris (rotenone), or quassia preparations, or beneficial insects. It is important to know that pyrethrum preparations are highly poisonous to human beings when they get into the bloodstream, when they come in contact with wounded skin, or when they get into open wounds. The pyrethrum extract is taken from the blossoms of *Chrysanthemum cinerariifolium*, which is planted in fields in Africa. It has an effect on the nervous system of insects and arthropods, but it is also dangerous to fish, although not to bees. Among the beneficial insects are: a small wasp, *Encarsia formosa*, useful in the fight against whitefly; predatory mites, *Phytoseiulus persimilis* to fight red spider mites and *Amblyseuis cucumeris* to fight thrips; predatory midges (*Aphidoletes*) and wasps (*Aphidius*) to fight greenfly (aphids). One can order these beneficial insects through the trade or by mail and let them loose in a closed room. As soon as they have eaten all their enemies, they die for lack of food. Beneficial insects can get rid of their enemies with fewer interruptions indoors than they can outdoors.

Chemical Protection

Chemicals have to be used precisely according to their instructions and at indicated dosage specifications. Under all circumstances, adhere to the recommended spraying intervals, in order to also destroy the following generations of parasites. Of course, one should not spray with environmentally damaging chemicals. One can only spray outdoors. Do not inhale the spray. Protect your hands with rubber gloves. Plant-protection sprays always should be kept in their original packaging and locked up, away from children and pets. If you have any leftovers, bring them to special hazardous garbage removal locations.

In the greenhouse, a closed cultivation room, it is possible to use helpful aids to fight against parasites. The yellow boards to which flying insect parasites stick are an example of nontoxic plant protection.

Yellow adhesive card to catch flying pests above a greenhouse table.

Physiological Diseases

Diseases that can occur, for example, in *Opuntia* because of too high air humidity, too low temperature, or too much nitrogen are called "corking," which results in unsightly brown spots and blotches starting at the base. Burns on the epidermis or red coloration of the upper skin and falling off of buds are results of too strong or changed incidence of light, respectively. Too high pH levels are especially dangerous for plants like *Cereus, Ferocactus, Lobivia,* and *Notocactus,* which do not like calcium.

Animal Pests

Greenfly (aphids) can be found, particularly on the buds of leaf cacti and at the ends of shoots of *Senecio* and other succulents. In a greenhouse or enclosed space, you can successfully use predatory midges and wasps to fight them. Besides that, you can use adhesive cards that they get stuck on or insecticides at intervals of 10–14 days.

Woodlice and mealy bugs: Place the plants in a cooler spot, carefully removing the white tufts that coat the insects with a brush and a spirit–soap solution (dissolve 1 splash of dishwater detergent in 1 quart (1 litre) water and add 1 tablespoon methylated spirits). Other possibilities: pyrethrum spray or other insecticides, white oils, Australian ladybugs (ladybirds).

Root mealy bugs are among the most dangerous parasites. They spin a mold-like, bluish-white wool around the roots. Check for this, when you repot! The plants turn yellow, grow only very poorly, and die. Dip the washed roots and all

planted pots repeatedly up to their top edges in insecticide solutions.

Root nematodes (eel worms): At the roots, particularly of cacti, *Euphorbia,* and *Kalanchoe,* are knotlike swellings and lemon-shaped, brownish cysts. The plants atrophy. Affected plants and infected soil must be destroyed, not composted; sterilize all pots, tools, etc., with heat.

Fungi, Bacteria, and Viruses

Powdery mildew fungus, with its white, flourlike growth, attacks *Euphorbia* and *Crassula* species, in particular. Remove the affected leaves and use a fungicide.

Fusarium rot (dry rot) is a fungus that discolors the vascular bundles and, after a wound, results in a soft rot with reddish to violet mold layers on the affected spots at the root neck or at the base of the sprout. Fight it with a fungicide; in the case of larger cultivations, also with *Bacillus subtilis,* a bacterium.

Phytophthora wet rot is a parasitic fungus that spreads from the infected soil to the roots. In plant bowls, the effect is disastrous. Only in the beginning stage can the affected spots be carefully cut out; later on, the only solution is radical destruction (burning) of the sick plants together with the soil. It is questionable whether a fungicide would be successful.

Helminthosporium wet rot mainly attacks young *Cereus, Echinocactus* and *Mammillaria,* at high air humidity and temperature. Causes: seed that wasn't dressed with a fungicide; soil that wasn't sterilized for sowing seed; an overly warm location of the sown

plants; and too high air humidity. Dark, glassy rot spots occur, which spread fast and soften the tissue. The plants fall over and dry out after a few days. Most of the time, every fight is hopeless; it is better to destroy the plants and the soil carefully. Do not put them into the compost!

Damping off. Cause/pathogenic agent: *Pythium, Rhizoctonia,* and others. Has an especially disastrous effect on seedlings and cuttings. Water with a fungicide.

Botrytis (grey mold). Occurs especially on weakened plants or on dead plant parts. Collections that are kept in airy and bright locations are rarely affected. Remove moldy leaves and plants. If need be, use fungicides.

Leaf spot causes sharply outlined, sunken, more or less circular, yellow-brown spots, which are often surrounded by dark red-brown circles. Cut out the affected areas, brush with spirits, and sprinkle with charcoal powder. Avoid high air humidity and high temperature.

Black rot, with blackening of the epidermis at or below soil level, occurs specifically in *Stapelia.* It is impossible to save them.

Brown coloration and corking, caused by fungi, are also found in *Aloe* and *Euphorbia* species.

Viruses and bacteria that attack certain *Epiphyllum* and *Rhipsalidopsis* species and wild *Opuntia* in Southern Europe, as well as the dwarf *Opuntia Tuna monstr.,* cannot be fought directly.

Safeguards for Succulents

Although succulents are robust plants, they are nevertheless not immune to diseases and pests. The best protection is prevention. Mistakes in care have to be avoided, and it's necessary to take a critical look at your plants from time to time.

Diseases

In contrast to other plants, which indicate that something is wrong with them by losing their leaves or by having discolored leaves, succulents often get sick without showing it. It is important, therefore, to recognize every sign of a disease early and to isolate sick plants immediately. Use a magnifying glass to help you. You will not only do better in discovering the location of the disease, but also the tiny evil-doers.

Physiological disorders, especially in the root area, are usually caused by mistakes in care, such as too warm overwintering, too much watering, overfertilizing or lack of nutrients, unsuccessful hardening, forgetting to repot, and dark or cool locations.

Fungi, viruses, and bacteria are also aided by mistakes in care, but they usually attack plants that are already sick. Susceptibility to disease depends on the state of development, on the generic disposition, and on the environmental conditions. Unfortunately, these diseases are contagious; an infection can quickly spread to an entire collection, especially since succulents usually stand close together or, when planted in bowls, share a common soil.

Pests

Animal pests rarely attack cacti and other succulents. The plants are protected against them because of

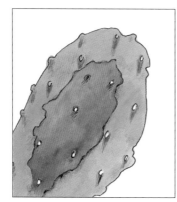

Sunburn. Symptoms: Brown-red spots, yellowish body. Remedy: Place plants in shade, especially in the spring and in the afternoon.

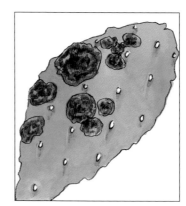

Corking. Symptoms: Brownish spots that spread. Remedy: Water less, air a lot; fertilize moderately.

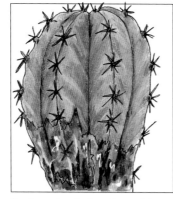

Root–neck rot. Symptoms: Discolored, glassy-rotten, fast-growing spots. Remedy: If the attack is already visible, one can only save the top of the plant.

Damping off of seedlings. Symptoms: Whitish web on the soil surface; glassy seedlings fall over. Remedy: Sterile conditions when sowing seeds, airing, use of fungicides.

their leathery, wax-coated, thick, exterior covering.

Most frequently, mealy bugs, root mealy bugs, and scales attack. In addition, there are red spider mites and, relatively seldom, nematodes. Snails actually only attack soft-fleshed succulents and juicy young plants. Other vermins like greenfly (aphids), thrips, ants, woodlice, worms, flies, caterpillars, etc. hardly play any roles. Animal pests are always brought in from the outside or fly in. Place new plants in quarantine for a couple of weeks. Only when it can be determined that they are not infected should they be placed with other plants.

Pest Control

When your succulents are sick or attacked by pests, do not use poisons immediately. First, try to fight the cause biologically, with useful insects, or with nonpoisonous chemical media like paraffin oil (white oil); soaplike products, for example based on potash salts; insecticides with active vegetable agents, or biotechnical control mediums, such as yellow flypaper cards. Inquire about suitable products at your plant stores, whose duty it is to give you advice. Only when everything has failed, and when you are dealing with an especially valuable plant, should a highly effective poison be used; one has to follow the instructions precisely also.

Red spider mites. *Symptoms: Pale plant bodies that are yellow-brown speckled, and scabby. Remedy: Fertilize preventively; use predatory mites or acaricides.*

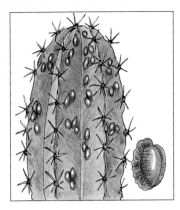

Scales. *Symptoms: Little brown scales, yellow sucking spots. Remedy: Australian ladybugs (ladybirds); insecticides.*

Mealy bugs. *Symptoms: Whitish, woolly, sticky, waxy excretions. Remedy: Same as for scales.*

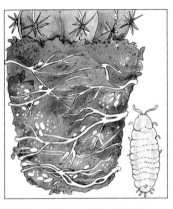

Root mealy bugs. *Symptoms: "Mold" at and around the roots. Remedy: Sterilize soil; water with insecticides.*

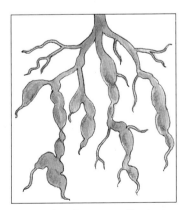

Nematodes. *Symptoms: Knots at the roots; shrivelled growth. Remedy: Destroy affected plants as well as the soil.*

Snails. *Symptoms: Eaten spots and slime traces on leaves. Remedy: Snail bait or other baits, traps, or fences.*

Index of Plant Names

Plants are listed here in
italics under their botanical
names and, if given in the
book, under their common
names. Bold type indicates
an illustration or photograph
of the plant on that page.

Subject Index

Photo Credits

Front cover photo: Epiphyllum Hybrid "Stern von Erlau," by Edi Day
Back cover: Left, Becherer; right, Nova.
Title page photo: Kleiner
Line illustrations by Ushie Dorner

Apel 30 l.
Becherer 51 u.r., 73 l., 92 t., u.l., and r., 129 (2), 133, 141, 151
Busek 56 m., 139
Eisenbeiss: 63 l.
Herbel 33 r., 39 l., 40 r., 41 l., 48 t.r., 49 m., 50 r., 53 l., 54 l., 90 l.
Hoffmann 81 l.

Kleiner 4 m., 37 l and r.; 38 l., 40 l., 42 (5), 43 u., 45 u.r., 46 m.l. and u.l.; 47 u.l., 53r., 55r., 56 l. and r., 60 m., 61 m., 62 m., 63 r., 64 l., 66 (2), 67 m., 70 l., 73 r., 77 l., 79, 81 r., 92 u.r., 93 l. and m., 94 l., 96 u.l., m.l. and r.; 100 t. and m., 101 u.l., 102 m., 103 m., 112 l., 115 u.m., 153
Leue 28/29, 46 t., m.r., u.r.; 47 t., m.l. and r., u.r.; 84/85, 135, 145
Melchert 136/137
Mosaik Zimmerpflanzen-Lexikon 45 t.
Nova 15 t.r., m.l., 34 r., 49 l., 62 r., 72 r., 78 r., 83

Rauh 4 u.r. and l., 13, 15 m., u., 21, 30 m. and r., 31, 32 l. and r., 33 l., 34 l., 35 r., 36 l., 39 l., 44 l., 48 l., 49 r., 50 l., 51 u.l., 52 l. and r., 53 m., 54 r., 55 l., 57 l., m., 58 r., 59 l. and r., 61 l. and r., 64 r., 65 l. and r., 67 r., 68 m. and r., 69 l. and r., 70 m., 71 (3), 74 l., 75 m. and r., 77 r., 78 l., 80 l. and r., 82 l. and r., 87 l., m., r., 88 r., 90 m. and r., 91 l. and m., 93 r., 94 m. and r., 95 r., 96 r., 97 l., m., r., 99 l. and r., 100 u.r., 101 m.r., 102 r., 103 l. and r., 104 m.l. and u.l., 106 t., m.l., u.l. and u.r., 107 l. and m., 108 r., 109 l. and r., 110 l. and r., 111 r., 113 m., 116 l. and r., 118 l. and r., 119 l. and r., 120 r., 121 (3).

Reinhard 6/7, 8/9, 11, 15 m.r., u.l., 19, 23, 35 l., 41 r., 57 r., 62 l., 68 l., 77 m., 96 t.
Smit 44 r., 48 mm., 98 r.
Stehling 91 r.
Tschakert 88 l., 122/123, 117
Welsch 125 u., 127
Wetterwald 5 t., 15 t.l. and u.r., 36 t., 38 r., 43 t., 51 t., 58 l., 60 r. and l., 67 l., 70 r., 74 r., 75 l., 76, 82 m., 86 (2), 89 l. and r., 95 l., 98 l., 100 u.l., 101 t., m.l. and r., 102 l., 104 t., m.r., and u.r., 105 (2), 107 r., 111 l., 112 r., 113 l., 114 t. and u., 115 (6), 120 l., 125 t., 131 (2), 143

Key: u, underneath; r, right; m, middle; l, left; m.l., middle left; t, top; t.r., top right; u.m., underneath, middle; m.r., middle right.

About the Author

Dr. Hans Hecht is a natural scientist, botanist, and phytopathologist, whose work at this time concentrates on horticulture. He leads a scientific test operation and is a member of the German Cactus Society (DKG) and of the International Organization for Succulent Plant Study (IOS), as well as the author of numerous trade publications. His long professional and private experience with succulent plants have made this book a useful handbook for both beginners and advanced cactus lovers.